To the Congregations of
St Saviour's, Guildford
1984-2009

David Bracewell is Rector of St. Saviour's Guildford, and Canon of Guildford Cathedral. Previously he was a Vicar in Bolton, following curacies in Tonbridge, Kent and Shipley, West Yorkshire. He has taught Pastoral Studies at Ridley Hall Cambridge and serves on the council of the 'Leaders of Larger Churches' network. He is married to Sue and they have three children and a granddaughter Zoë, with a second grandchild expected imminently.

15 Minutes to Wake the Dead

A Selection of Sermons by
DAVID BRACEWELL

Gentle encouragement for becalmed preachers and bewildered congregations

Published by Zoë Ministry

We want to hear from you. Please send your comments about this book to us at
david@zoeministry.co.uk

15 Minutes to Wake the Dead
A Selection of Sermons by David Bracewell
Gentle encouragement for becalmed preachers and bewildered congregations

By David Bracewell
Copyright © 2009 by David Bracewell

ISBN 978-0-9564114-0-2

Published by Zoë Ministry
www.zoeministry.co.uk

Requests for further information or copies of this book should be sent to
Zoë Ministry, St Saviour's, Woodbridge Road, Guildford, Surrey GU1 4QD

Illustrations by Ron Wood & Huw Briscoe, Copyright © 2009
Cover and interior designed by Big Pond Design

Printed in the United Kingdom

Contents

This is how it happened

I have a cartoon in my study of a rather harassed man sitting at his desk surrounded by piles of books and papers. In the doorway his wife, arms folded, is looking accusingly. The man is turning to face her and the caption reads: 'Finish it? Why would I want to finish it?'

I have been attempting to write a book for years, and my efforts have become a sort of family joke. From time to time, sitting at my desk, I have caught members of the family sniggering and nudging each other: 'He's at the book again. He'll never finish it.' Well, in a sense they were right. This is not the book I've been trying to write for years. But it **is** a book and I **have** finished it. So there!

This is how it happened. About a year ago a young man who used to be a member of our congregation, and is now a curate in Bristol, suggested that I commit some of my sermons to print. I dismissed the idea at first, but then it began to grow on me. My original thought was to do something fairly simple and offer it to the congregation as a sort of double-edged leaving present as I prepared to retire: a memento of what we had been through together over 25 years. But then I began to talk to a couple of people at St Saviour's who persuaded me that this would be worth doing properly – a real book rather than sheaves of stapled paper. Moreover they told me they had the contacts and expertise to make it happen. So, after six months of reflecting, transcribing, editing and generally making a nuisance of myself to all involved – here it is.

The book divides into four sections: sermons preached on special occasions, at major festivals, on particular topics and on incidents from John's gospel. As I worked on them I discovered they fell into two categories. First, there were those, usually quite brief, that had been written word for word and then delivered from memory. They are quite precise, and it took no time to edit the transcripts. They are mostly contained in sections 1 and 3. And secondly, there were the longer sermons, to my own congregation, delivered from outline notes. When I received the transcribed texts of these I was appalled at how random and loosely structured they were. To edit them into written form was a major undertaking.

Although the sermons have been tidied up, I have tried to retain something of the immediacy of the spoken word. The sermon is an act of live communication, rather than a polished piece of reflection, although at its best it can be both. For myself, much work goes into the thoughts expressed, and into the structure that carries those thoughts – but the delivery is fairly spontaneous.

I have retained quite a few local and personal references. From time to time the name 'Gordon' appears. Gordon is a treasured friend, and an enthusiastic listener. He sits right at the front with his wife Tess, and whenever I become a bit excited I tend to address Gordon directly, and through him the whole congregation. In one sense Gordon is a 'fall guy', but at a deeper level he incarnates the principle of preaching as partnership. Over the years he has inspired me, more than he will ever know, to try to preach well.

The biblical quotations are from the NIV unless otherwise stated. Now and again I paraphrase the text of Scripture to bring it into a contemporary setting. These flights of fancy have been italicized in the text, to distinguish them from Scripture itself. I hope the book is one which the reader can dip into over a period of time. To read 24 sermons at one sitting would be an unimaginable act of masochism.

I have a lot of people to thank. First of all, James Stevenson who believed enough in my preaching to suggest it deserved a wider audience. He is the person to thank as you read on. I am so grateful for his enthusiasm, wisdom and friendship as we have shaped this project together. His father, Kenneth, until recently Bishop of Portsmouth, has provided a gracious foreword.

I want to thank Richard Dunning who with gentle wit and subversive determination persuaded me to do a proper book and paved the way with his skills and practical know-how. Andy Southan has put the whole thing together and prepared it for publication with wonderful skills and generosity. Without his work, nothing would have ever happened. A noble army of typists/martyrs, led by Jennie McDuff, valiantly offered to listen to CDs of the sermons and transcribe them into print: a labour of love indeed. Cary Gilbart-Smith did valiant work in checking the text with meticulous care making sure it made sense - both grammatically and theologically.

I want to thank also the writers of the 'View from the Pew' pieces. They are all faithful members of St Saviour's and have sat patiently through countless sermons. I am grateful for their generous comments, wise insights – and terrifying expectations! They are representative of all who Sunday by Sunday shape the life of the preacher (and the sermon) by their attentive listening. I have had the luxury of two cartoonists. The cartoons in the main text are by Ron Wood. His regular contributions to the Church Times are a delight and I am grateful to him for generously providing me with some examples of his skill. The four cartoons at the head of each section have been drawn by Huw Briscoe who was until recently a member of St Saviour's, and is now beginning a career as a graphic artist. He has a great future ahead!

Special thanks are due to Anna, my PA, who has brought the whole project together with great speed, patience and skill. She also happens to be my daughter, which means that I have not received any of the deference usually expected of a PA, but on the other hand she has been ruthless in rebuking my vagueness, interpreting my handwritten scrawl and making sure I didn't let things drift. She is a star!

Finally, I owe a debt of gratitude to my wife, Sue. She is the one who gave me the cartoon that hangs in my study and she has been patient (most of the time) as I have laboured distractedly on the book. Her love, wisdom and down-to-earth honesty sustain me day by day. I suspect much of her encouragement for this project is because she thinks my book-writing obsession is now at an end. What she doesn't know is that, with my customary naïve optimism, I'm thinking it might just be the beginning!

Foreword

I first knew David Bracewell in the Manchester Diocese in the early 1980s but only got to know him properly later on when we were neighbours in Guildford for almost a decade.

There had been a history of nervousness between St Saviour's, a large evangelical parish, and the town centre civic parish of Holy Trinity. But we made friends and even managed to 'swap pulpits', as the saying goes.

I always enjoyed his preaching. It was invariably simple, deep, with lively illustrations that were never trite, and they always used humour. On one occasion I pointed him out to a new Archdeacon with the words, 'He's the best preacher in the Guildford Diocese.' Even though we come from different traditions, we both value the interplay of Scripture, human experience, and prayer – combined with hard thinking and soft feeling.

You can't listen to David's sermons without being aware of two underlying dimensions. They are always worth listening to, and they are always the result of a great deal of time and care. Perhaps it's that combination of time and care that makes him worth listening to in the first place. Those who are over-enthusiastic to get into the pulpit perhaps need to approach their task with more humility.

I'm glad that he has been persuaded – by our son, James, a former parishioner of his – to put some of these 'winged words' into published form. They will carry you into new realms – and help you see new vistas of God's eternal Kingdom!

Bishop Kenneth Stevenson, Former Bishop of Portsmouth

Introduction

And a young man named Eu'tychus was sitting in the window. He sank into a deep sleep as Paul talked still longer; and being overcome by sleep, he fell down from the third storey and was taken up dead.
(Acts 20.9)

John Ruskin's view of the sermon as '15 minutes to wake the dead', assumes that it is the congregation who have expired, and the preacher is the heroic figure working a miracle of resurrection – week after week.[1] But what if it is the person in the pulpit who is dead (or half-alive) and it is the listeners who are cast in the role of miracle-workers? It is true that many congregations seem instinctively resistant to preaching, whatever its quality, but on the other hand my own experience leads me to believe that Sunday by Sunday all over Britain congregations are rendered comatose by inadequate preaching.[2]

What is the cause of this malaise, whether in pulpit or pew? I have come to believe that at root it is a deep resistance to the personal renewal that authentic preaching will always demand. The chorus of women in T.S. Eliot's Murder in the Cathedral speak of the apathy with which all of us are plagued from time to time, not least when we are challenged to change:

> *We do not wish anything to happen.*
> *Seven years we have lived quietly,*
> *Succeeded in avoiding notice,*
> *Living and partly living[3]*

The conviction that underlies this book is that the sermon is a partnership between preacher and congregation in which heart, mind and will are engaged on both sides. When the preacher is doing his or her job well, new spiritual possibilities are opened up within those who hear, and in turn energy then flows back to the preacher. A dynamic partnership is set up whereby the Word of God becomes alive, active and transformative.[4]

So let's begin with the **preacher**, for it is here that the initiative lies. Until someone has stood up and started to speak there is no sermon. The preacher has two tools with which to work, namely the text of Scripture and his own personality, and both need to be handled with skill and integrity if the sermon is to be effective.

The handling of the text is an awesome task. Those who preach are commissioned by God, and authorised by the Church, so to expound Scripture that human words become the vehicle for the divine Word taking root in the lives of those who hear, effecting spiritual transformation. Christ makes himself present in the preaching. John Wesley records in his journal an occasion when he preached to thousands of miners gathered on a hillside outside Bristol: 'I offered them Christ for the space of two hours.' I bet no one fell asleep!

Where the text is mishandled, ignored or used as a launch-pad for other agendas, all the congregation has left is the ideas of the preacher. 'I thought this morning I would just say a few words about...' The words may be profound, or not, but, unrelated to the eternal Word, they will have no power to save. To say this is to state the obvious, and simply raises a whole host of further questions, the primary one being, 'How can I effectively expound this text?' The answer may be, and for many still is, through a detailed verse-by-verse analysis. It is a method I employed for years, but of late it has worried me. As well as producing very long sermons, it can unwittingly trap both preacher and congregation in a first century time-capsule. It need not be so of course, but the temptation somehow seems inherent in the method.

This sort of sermon is all text, often delivered with an earnest desire to convey biblical truth at all costs, but not obviously passing through the prism of the preacher's own experience, and so not effectively rooted in the realities of daily life. Here preaching is turned into lecture mode with information handed down, requiring the congregation simply to listen and learn. The possibilities of real dialogue are lost. The poet, R.S. Thomas tells of a young Welsh deacon reflecting on his early attempts at preaching:

> *They listened to me preaching the unique gospel*
> *Of love, but our eyes never met.* [5]

If preaching is to be transformative, eyes must meet. I have listened to many sermons, and to my shame preached some, that could have been awarded top marks for orthodox content, and clarity of structure, but left the congregation saying, 'So what?' My wife who is my fiercest and therefore most prized critic, will often say, 'Please, in your sermon tell us what we have to do.' If I were allowed only one sentence to offer to a room full of aspiring preachers I would say, 'Please, root your sermon in the life of your hearers.' Most of the sermons that follow are not expository in the traditional sense (Nos. 5 & 9 would be an exception), but I would want to claim that they are thoroughly biblical. What merit they have is for you, dear reader, to judge but they have come out of painstaking attention to the text and, above all, a costly exercise of the imagination. Before he stands in the pulpit the preacher ought to have dismantled the text for understanding, examined it for application, and reassembled it for communication. Exegesis, hermeneutics and homiletics are the technical terms, but they all add up to plain hard work to produce the sort of sermon that may appear to sit lightly to the text but is in fact marinated in Scripture.

The second tool at the preacher's disposal is his own personality. The challenge here is for him to be vulnerable, which is not the same as being constantly autobiographical. He must have the courage to stand with the congregation under the authority of the text. Not 'This is what you must do,' or 'This is what I think,' but 'This is what the text requires of us all.' I remember once preaching in a theological college chapel, and afterwards one of the tutors coming to me and saying, 'Listening to you I thought, "I could tell that man anything." ' It was one of the most humbling and encouraging comments I have ever received. Where there is vulnerability, connection is made between preacher and congregation and genuine dialogue becomes possible. Deep speaks to deep and things can begin to happen in the realm of the Spirit. By contrast, where there is no attempt to make connection the results are fatal, and can be hilarious. Evelyn Waugh has a great moment in his novel, A Handful of Dust, when he introduces the Reverend Tendril, Vicar of Hatton and Compton Last. For years the Vicar has preached his sermons in a garrison chapel in India. Now, deep in rural England, the same sermons are delivered with no attempt at adaptation. His Christmas sermon never varied:

> 'How difficult it is for us,' he began, blandly surveying his congregation, who coughed into their mufflers, and chafed their chilblains under their woollen gloves, 'to realise that this is indeed Christmas. Instead of the glowing log fire and the windows tight shuttered against the drifting snow, we have only the harsh glare of an alien sun; instead of the happy circle of loved faces, of home and family, we have the uncomprehending stares of the subjugate, though no doubt grateful, heathen. Instead of the placid ox and ass of Bethlehem,' said the Vicar, slightly losing the thread of his comparisons, 'we have for companions the ravening tiger and the exotic camel, the furtive jackal and the ponderous elephant...' And so on, through pages of faded manuscripts.' [6]

This is an extreme example of course, but there is just enough truth here to give cause for concern. The preacher must keep asking, 'What is this eternal Word saying to this particular congregation at this moment?' The German theologian and preacher, Helmut Thielicke, said, 'The Gospel must constantly be forwarded to a new address.' Faithfulness to the ancient Word always requires that it be addressed to the contemporary scene. If you are a preacher I suggest it might be worth pinning Thielicke's advice to the surface of your desk. And because we are talking about passion to connect, I recall another pithy sentence delivered by Douglas Cleverly Ford, who was for many years Principal of the College of Preachers: 'The unpardonable sin in preaching is to bore people.' That too was fastened to the top of my desk, until it became too uncomfortable to live with!

The other side of this partnership is the **congregation**. Too often it is assumed that their contribution to the task of preaching is to sit passively and take what comes; the sermon is something done to them, often by someone from whom they do not deserve such treatment! Nothing could be further from the truth. The sermon is not a missive aimed at the congregation, it is a creative dialogue initiated by the preacher on behalf of the congregation, an invitation to explore together wide vistas of theological truth and practical discipleship. This partnership depends on mutual trust. A congregation may never feel safe (after all we are meeting the God who is described as a consuming fire) but it needs to feel secure. Secure in the hands of God, but secure also in the hands of the preacher – theologically and emotionally. Where the preacher replaces truth with novelty, determined to shock rather than teach, an uneasy mood will be created. If there is emotional pressure, manipulation or threat, a congregation will freeze. And trust takes time. So I would want to say that the most satisfying preaching is pastoral preaching. I take my hat off to itinerant preachers (and on the edge of 'retirement' I suppose I am about to become one) but there is no substitute for standing Sunday by Sunday among a group of people whose lives you know, whose joys and sorrows you have shared, whose anger you have at times roused and then absorbed, whose children you have baptised and married and whose loved ones you have laid to rest, offering them Christ who is sufficient for every need.

So what is the role of the congregation? Although not a regular member of one I would make bold to say: 'when you come to church, and more especially to the preaching of the Word, come as a shaper, come as a learner, come as a dreamer.[7]

Come as a **shaper** for you have so much to give. R.S. Thomas's Welsh deacon castigated himself for lacking the courage to look his people in the eye, but I have faced many a congregation who seem prepared to look anywhere except at the preacher. There is a sense in which the congregation gets the preacher it deserves. Eyes must meet, the congregation needs to look, to listen and to expect. And, if the preacher seems to be struggling, to pray. Perhaps above all to speak – although not if possible while the sermon is in progress!

What happens after the sermon has been delivered is of vital importance. When I worked in the North of England the congregation, if unhappy with what I had said, would pin me to the door on the way out. It was painful, but at least I knew where I stood. In the Home Counties it is more genteel – the rapier rather than the sledge hammer. From time to time I receive a carefully crafted letter, or a thoughtful word of encouragement or rebuke. Perhaps the best contribution a congregation can make is to register moments when a sermon has brought real change: a situation is resolved, a fear overcome, a vision planted, a doubt resolved. The Word of God, faithfully preached, reaches deep into someone's life as a link is suddenly made between the ancient text and some contemporary dilemma. Bishop Peter Firth illustrates this point well:

Every Christian congregation can write new chapters in this unfolding story. In any local church – and the wider community it serves – there is a Moses who speaks and an Aaron who follows; there is a Peter who denies and a Thomas who doubts; there is an over-passionate David and a Susannah who values her virginity as a gift from God. There is an Ezra with a building vision and a Mary who watches and prays. There are Jacobs who wrestle with God all night in prayer and Amos's who fight for justice. The list is endless.[8]

It is important that these moments of identification and transformation be spoken about, and, where appropriate, rehearsed within the congregation. When this happens the effect on both congregation and preacher can be remarkable, and can often raise a corporate sense of expectation about what God might do next.

Come as a **learner**, for you have much to receive. The contribution of the congregation begins long before the sermon is delivered. In my own church we are about to embark on a series of sermons on the Epistle to the Ephesians and I have just sent a note to the congregation urging them to get one step ahead of the preacher by spending some time in the text of Ephesians before the series starts. We have on sale a few basic commentaries and some bible reading notes. We have four congregations and they will all be studying the same material, as also will our midweek cell groups (apart from one or two rogue ones which always do their own thing). These groups, which are far wider and deeper than just study groups, will chew over the material in the previous week's sermon. All these are small things, but cumulatively they serve to give a sense that we are all in this business of wrestling with Ephesians together. The joy and the pain are shared! Among many other things the sermon provides biblical information, and every preacher is encouraged by hearers who do want to learn and grow in knowledge and faith. But we gather not just for information, but for understanding and for wisdom so that we might live well.

Happy the preacher whose congregation long to grow up in Christ. At this deep level we all need to come as learners.

> *Where is the life we have lost in living?*
> *Where is the wisdom we have lost in knowledge?*
> *Where is the knowledge we have lost in information.*[9]

Finally, come as a **dreamer**, for you have so much to experience. There are moments during the sermon when the Holy Spirit seems to inhabit afresh the human word so that something shifts in the consciousness of all involved. The Canadian Pastor and preacher, Loren B. Mead describes it well.

> *There is a moment early in the preaching event in which some deep parts of the listener are opened up to the preacher as one is not routinely opened to a neighbour or a friend or even a spouse. That moment is an invitation to transformation and an opportunity for a dialogue from depth to depth.*[10]

Such moments are precious, but so fragile. They cannot be engineered, or even anticipated, but they are to be received with gratitude and acted upon with courage. It requires only that people come with their dreams of how life might be under the reign and rule of God, and with a real expectation that He will meet them and respond to their longings.

> *Come down, O love divine,*
> *seek thou this soul of mine,*
> *and visit it with thine own ardour glowing.*

Then the moment of transformation comes which makes all the listening and all the speaking worthwhile. We have spoken of two actors in the drama of preaching, but of course there is a third, without whose presence nothing will happen. Jesus said, 'When the Spirit of truth comes, he will guide you into all the truth... He will teach you everything, and remind you of all that I have said to you.' (John 16.13; 14.25) In preaching, everything diligently studied, carefully prepared and skilfully delivered must be laid open to the coming of the **Spirit of God**, for unless our thinking, speaking and listening are touched by his fire everything will be cold and lifeless.

That heavenly Teacher, sent from God,
Shall your whole soul inspire;
Your mind shall fill with sacred truth,
Your hearts with sacred fire. (Scottish paraphrase)

Fifteen minutes to wake the dead? Well maybe, but what about: 'Fifteen minutes to kindle a fire that will burn on from heart to heart, bringing transformation to preacher and congregation, hope to a broken world, and glory to God.

1. Often attributed to John Ruskin.
2. This sounds harsh, and my experience is limited, but it would seem to be confirmed by what others say.
3. T.S. Eliot, Murder in the Cathedral, pt.1.
4. Keeping up He/She is tiresome so I have kept to he (being a man!) But she is always implied. I am a great believer in women's ministry and in their preaching powers.
5. R.S. Thomas, 'The Minister', Collected poems 1945-1990, (Pheonix Giants, 1993).
6. Evelyn Waugh, A Handful of Dust, (Penguin, 1997) p.61.
7. These headings were suggested by a chapter in J.V. Taylor's book 'A Matter of Life and Death' (SCN, 1986).
8. From an article by Peter Firth in the Bible Society magazine 'Transmission', (Autumn 1997) p.14.
9. T.S.Eliot, Choruses from 'The Rock'.
10. Loren B. Mead, 'Transforming Congregations for the Future, (Alban Institute, 1994) p.56.

Part 1

Engagement

The evening service proved a real hit with the struggling insomniacs

'A survey of British churchgoers discovered that some 42% of them admitted to falling asleep in church. More than a third looked at their watch every Sunday, and an amazing 10% owned up to putting their watch to their ear and shaking it, because they thought it must have stopped.'

(John Drane)

This is the shortest sermon I have ever delivered! My mandate was seven minutes, but it probably took no more than five.

Preaching in the setting of a school assembly or college chapel is one of the most terrifying experiences imaginable. 'Five minutes in which to wake the dead.' On the odd occasion that I am still asked, I always say yes – and then invariably regret it as the day approaches.

The physical structure of Charterhouse Chapel, though magnificent, presents an enormous communication challenge. 750 pupils face each other in tiered ranks as far as the eye can see with the pulpit high up half way down the north side of the chapel. Building a relationship is a non-starter!

The text was a long reading from the Passion story as told by St John around which I tried to gather the thread of the sermon. The challenge is to gain attention immediately and then hold it for those few precious moments.

I felt it was an abject failure, but over a convivial supper after the service, the Chaplain urged me to believe that it had worked. His trained eye was able to pick up tiny signals that the customary boredom had been replaced by a flicker of attentiveness. I can only take his word for it.

Nonetheless to preach the unsearchable riches of Christ in such a setting is a wonderful privilege.

1.Gerbil or Rebel?

The other day I bought a bottle of white wine from Marks & Spencer. On the reverse of the label were these words: 'Be passionate, love, dream big, change the world, or go home.' The wine was ok, but I would have paid double just to get the label.

What are you passionate about?

Some time ago, my family, worn down by my constant nagging, bought me a small and fairly old sports car. They think I look quite sad in it, but I don't care. I'm passionate about it. Every time I drive it I get a buzz of excitement. I'm a passionate pensioner.

There are two ways of being passionate

You can be passionate about your own well-being, driving yourself to achievement: wealth, education, career, family. Or you can be passionate about a cause outside of yourself: justice, freedom, care for the sick, ecology. The passions are not mutually exclusive, of course. But if you embrace the first and neglect the second, you will diminish yourself. You may end up living like a gerbil. You go to work, to earn the money, to buy the food, to make you strong, to go to work .... Round and round an endless circle. But if you focus on the second, the first will come as well, slipping in by the back door so to speak. Giving yourself to something, or someone, beyond yourself, will bring hope to the world and all the self-fulfilment you can handle. In our self-obsessed culture you will become a rebel. Think Geldof and Hope for African children, think Bono and the alleviation of poverty, think Mandela and the pursuit of justice.

Think Jesus Christ, a man of passion. "The Passion of the Christ". He was the ultimate rebel coming not just to save the world but to change it, not by force but through love. Not leading an army, but nailed to a cross. Contrast the other characters in tonight's reading. Peter concerned to save his own skin, Pilate terrified of his wife, the priests clinging on to power and status. And in the middle, standing firm, strong and true: Jesus Christ - a rebel with a cause. For 50 years I have stumblingly tried to follow him, and I get more passionate about him every day.

> *Though giant rains put out the sun,*
> *Here stand I for a sign.*
> *Though earth be filled with waters dark,*
> *My cup is filled with wine.*
> *Tell to the trembling priests that here*
> *Under the deluge rod,*
> *One nameless, tattered, broken man*
> *Stood up, and drank to God!* [1]

That's G. K. Chesterton. I'm not absolutely sure what it means, but the mood of magnificent defiance is very clear.

So, life as a gerbil or a rebel?

The choice, ladies and gentlemen, is yours.

1. G.K. Chesterton, 'The Deluge'.

View from the Pew

What do I hope for in a sermon? I have to remind myself that to expect the preacher to feed me, 'entertain' me, meet some sort of expectation – other than hearing from God - is not what it's all about, and yet I can so easily do that.

It is, rather, a two-way thing. I must be willing to hear, to receive, to think! I suppose what I most appreciate from a sermon is relevant truth. Even when it's hard-hitting and I'm left less than comfortable. Obviously we need encouragement, but I can often find that in God's Word and from fellow Christians. Somewhere I need to be exhorted and challenged. How wonderful those moments when my spirit says 'Yes!' even when I may not particularly like what I'm hearing! If I feel irritated, even angered, I am the one who should explore why I am reacting that way before judging the preacher. I want/need to trust that he or she has been anointed and spoken to by God, so I can hear Him speaking to me through the man or woman He has chosen to have 'up front'.

Yet at the same time I know we mustn't expect to be spoon-fed; how great it is when we are made to think – to want to go away and continue exploring, praying around the subject! 'A sermon should lead us to pursue greater understanding, launch a search, agitate us...' (Jeff Lucas). But then what I do with that truth is not the responsibility of the preacher. My role is to take, follow through, trust, obey and act on what God has said.

The method of delivery can of course play an enormous part. Humour and storytelling are vital (something Jesus used in His teaching!), along with honesty and vulnerability that engages the congregation and enables us in turn to engage with the teaching.

Sue Wavre

Weddings are, by definition,
joyful occasions.

People are 'dressed to the nines,' relaxed and talkative,
although often not far beneath the surface there are
moments of tension and sometimes sadness, as this sermon
acknowledges. I think it is important to keep the sermon
brief, personal and light (although not theologically
lightweight). I have sat through many wedding sermons
(and have preached some) that have been long and rather
earnest biblical expositions of the Christian understanding
of marriage. On the whole, they
miss the mark.

Something needs to be said that will root iself in the hearts
of the couple being married, resonate with Christians
supporting them, and give food for thought to those who
know nothing of the Faith and for whom attendance at
a church is an alien (and even a rather nerve-wracking)
experience. It is a tall order, requiring sensitivity, a passon
to make connection and a lightness of touch. Oh dear!

This wedding involved two much-loved members of the
church – that makes it easier. Other situations can be much
more difficult, of course, and will require very great care.

2.James & Nicky

When it comes to choosing readings for weddings, couples fall into three categories. First of all those who choose obvious readings for simple reasons. It may be that they are unused to being in church, it may be they know very little of the Bible and so they go for obvious passages that come back to their memory, something like Psalm 23 and 1 Corinthians 13. Then, secondly, there are people who choose unusual readings for what they believe to be obvious reasons. These are Christian couples and they will go to the Old Testament, or to the complex Pauline epistles of Ephesians and Colossians, because they know a lot about the Bible. Sometimes this requires the preacher to do some theological gymnastics because the passages chosen are often not about marriage, but that's another issue. The third category is peopled by James and Nicky alone, who have chosen obvious passages for complex and deeply theological reasons.

My slight problem at the moment is that I've forgotten what those reasons are. We did talk about it a long time ago, so I suspect that at some point after this sermon there will be a theological post mortem. But then, what's new, James?! All is well, because we know each other. I love you guys, I feel so privileged to be invited to take part in this special day. It really is an enormous honour. Incidentally, if you ever feel tempted to doubt my care for you, will you remember that, about one month after General Synod decreed that all public services should be addressed by clergy wearing appropriate robes, I was willing to defy that in the presence of, I think, no fewer than three bishops?[1] They are everywhere! It is the stuff of nightmares!

(At this point Bishop Kenneth Stevenson, father of the bridegroom, interrupted the Sermon. He is a larger-than-life character and we know each other fairly well, so it was all good fun. The brief interjection went as follows:

Bishop Kenneth: 'David, **you** are the nightmare!'

David: 'It's an absolute delight and privilege to have you here, your eminence. Shy and retiring as ever!')

Now what was I saying? The first reading was Psalm 23:'The Lord is my shepherd, I shall not be in want, he makes me to lie down in green pastures, he leads me beside quiet waters, he restores my soul.' It is so beautiful, it is so pastoral, it is so comforting that sometimes we are blinded to the radical, sharp, cutting edge of that text. To be a shepherd is not an easy or simple task. A shepherd's love involves commitment, toil, endurance, sacrifice. It is gritty, practical love.

And then 1 Corinthians 13, 'If I speak in the tongues of men and of angels but have not love, I am only a resounding gong or a clanging cymbal.' Again, the well-loved words can conceal a very radical edge. Listen to the words of this chapter in a modern translation!

> *The love of which I speak is slow to lose patience, it looks for a way of being constructive, it is not possessive, it is neither anxious to impress, nor does it cherish inflated ideas of its own importance.*

Put that into the context of a marriage (or a church meeting?) and it's a bombshell!

> *Love has good manners and does not pursue selfish advantage. It is not touchy, it does not keep account of evil or gloat over the wickedness of other people; on the contrary, it is glad when the truth prevails. Love knows no limit to its endurance, no end to its trust, no fading of its hope, it can outlast anything, it is*

in fact the one thing that still stands when all else has fallen.
(J.B. Phillips)

James and Nicky, you are bringing yourselves on your wedding day under the costly care and love of the Good Shepherd, who already owns your allegiance. And you know that the Good Shepherd's love endures for ever. It will never fail you or forsake you. He loves you even to death upon a cross. And it will always be there, or rather, He will always be there. Because it is Christ whose love 'knows no limit to its endurance, no end to its trust, no fading of its hope, Christ's love can outlast anything; it is in fact the one thing that still stands when all else has fallen.' So we rejoice with you today that you are rooted and grounded in Christ, that you are coming afresh to affirm that allegiance, to acknowledge that he is your shepherd, your Lord, your guide and your friend.

But there is another aspect to the passage. The New Testament likens us to sheep but it also challenges us to be shepherds after the pattern of Christ, the chief shepherd. So in reading these passages, not only are you opening yourselves once again to receive the love and care of Christ, but you are offering yourselves to be shepherds, to look after the flock of God, wherever that might be in the days ahead. You are promising to open your eyes, your minds and your hearts to a broken world, where you will pastor in the name of Christ. So the readings are both a gift and a commission. And we rejoice with you in that double blessing and pray for God's presence to go with you.

James and Nicky this is for you, but actually everyone here is included. For some of us, weddings are bittersweet moments because we are so happy for this new marriage, but we have known brokenness and failure and sadness. You may be on your own after a fractured relationship. You may be trying to build again. You may at this very moment be undergoing enormous strain in a relationship, almost to the point of breaking. Today I want you to know that because of Christ it is always possible to start again, and I want to invite us all to rekindle our relationships with the fire of God's love. Its a fierce fire that burns up all that is unreal, untrue and unfaithful and prepares us for new and radical living. Together may we bring our lives under that radical love of the Good Shepherd, and know that as we abide in Christ there is healing for all our wounds, renewal for all our sadness and hope for all the future.

Nicky and James, God's richest blessing on you! James I love you. I love your passion for God, which is so rooted in truth, integrity and clarity. I look forward to hundreds of theological postmortems of my sermons. And Nicky? I love you just because you're Nicky. We have, I think, a special relationship. If I were thirty years younger, and five inches taller... and unmarried... who knows?! But you have been to me, over the years, an endless source of encouragement and joy and so it's a delight to be at your wedding. And I pray that as you go out from this church, and as you begin to build your lives together after the pattern of the Good Shepherd, whose wounded love will lead you all your days, your home and your lives will be an image of God's eternal Kingdom. The God to whom be ascribed, as is most justly due, all might, majesty, dominion and power, henceforth and for evermore, Amen.

1. Date of the wedding was December 2002

"I hate it when this happens,"
said Toby

This sermon was preached at the funeral of a much-loved and elderly member of the congregation.

Not a hard task. I have preached at the funerals of children, teenagers, students, people estranged from the church, people suddenly lost through illness or accident, and that is a very different matter and an enormous challenge.

Brief facts about the person's life need to be assembled, and if they can be memorised and delivered without reference to notes that really helps to convey a sense of care. Sometimes these facts are delivered by a relative or friend in a tribute.

Interwoven with the biographical material will be some spiritual reflection; this can be difficult if the preacher is unsure of the deceased's relationship to the Faith. Honesty and sensitivity are required in equal measure and of course it is not always an evasion to say that the state of a person's soul, especially as death approaches, is known to God alone.

I think the best sequence of events for a Christian funeral is for the crematorium service to happen first (usually attended only by relatives and close friends) followed immediately by a service of thanksgiving in church. This sermon was preached at such a service of thanksgiving.

3.Mary

The outward events of Mary's life, which we celebrate today, are simply and briefly told. She was brought up in Norwood, where she taught for a while. Then the family moved to Godalming, in fact to Milford. Her father was Professor of Chemistry at St. Thomas's Hospital and the teaching department moved down here. Then war broke out, and Mary got a job, in the GPO in North Street in Guildford, where she met Marguerite Durrant, and so began a life-long friendship. Then after a brief time back in London the family settled here permanently. She taught at Gosden House in Bramley. The headmistress there, Miss Beryl Rook, can't be here today but she wanted you to know what a splendid career Mary had there, and how she touched the lives of very many people, particularly a lady called Joan. They met first when they were five years old at primary school. I don't think Joan will mind if I tell you that she is 88, so that's a friendship of 83 years which is something quite remarkable. Mary lived in William Road and was later the Receptionist at Dapdune Surgery, which is where I first met her. These are the simple facts, very straightforward and very easily told.

But what about the woman herself? Well, first of all I want to say that she had **style**. She was, for a woman of her generation, quite tall and I used to watch her, before she became much more frail, walking down the corridor in Church. She was like a galleon in full sail! She had a marvellous telephone manner. She would ring me up and say 'Good morning Rector – Miss Lowndes here'. And I would say 'Good morning Miss Lowndes, how splendid to hear you!' She was gracious, regal and rather an awesome character. She had style, but she had **a warm heart**. She had a vast network of family and friends who she loved and who she kept in touch with over the years. She seemed to have a remarkable ability just to keep the contacts going. Early in our friendship I heard about her Canadian relatives whom she visited regularly. We are so glad to see you here today: cousin Julian and wife Catherine, and son Geoff and grandson Mitchell, and cousin Rachel. It's wonderful to have you all here. And then the friends – so many of them. The Durrant family who were like a family to her here in Guildford, Marguerite and Ken, Anne and Dudley and your children; it's been good to talk to you and discover how much she was part of your life, and of all that you did for her. And of course Gerald Williams, who she taught as a little boy in Norwood, and then, seeing him commentating at Wimbledon, she wrote to him at the BBC, and Gerald phoned and they've been firm friends ever since.

So - a splendid style, and a warm heart, but also **an open mind**. This is so important to record. People of a certain generation can get very locked into traditional ways and become dismissive of new things. The remarkable thing about Mary was that she spanned the generations. My last youth pastor and my present one, Andy Emerton and Phil Mann, are both here today; sparky young post-modern men who were remarkably close to Mary. They have said to me: 'Mary was so important to us, she was so vibrant, so concerned about the younger generation, so supportive of our work, so open.' That is a remarkable thing and I commend it to you – the ability to span the generations and to hold them together. Young people, seemingly so competent and technologically brilliant, are very often adrift and needing mentors. Mary was such a person.

Latterly she served on the Welcome Desk at church. She said to me: 'I shall never give that up until I really have to', and right until her rather unexpected death on December 21st, she was doing her duty on that desk. I would see her and say, 'Good morning Miss Lowndes.' And she would say, 'Good Morning Rector!'

So the style was splendid, the heart was warm, the mind was open and **finally the faith was simple** – not simplistic, but simple. In company with many of her generation she didn't talk about it. She would say things about my sermons, and sometimes they were complimentary! In fact I sensed of late an opening up of her spiritual understanding. We listened to a song in the crematorium sung by Jonathan Veira, 'May you go peacefully, may you be known by love.' She did and she was. She had an enormous compassion and care for people – love which is patient, which is kind, which is not rude, which does not boast, all those things that come in I Corinthians, chapter 13. She had a faith which issued in love, which was then expressed in practical ways – and I can see you nodding even as I speak, for you have been recipients of her care and her magnificent love.

But a love, of course, which in this life is never complete, because 'Now we see through a glass darkly, but then face to face! Now I know in part – then I shall know fully even as I have been fully known.' I Corinthians, chapter 13.12. And now Mary stands – complete in the presence of Christ whom she loved and served. I think if in heaven there is a reception desk with a telephone, she may well at this moment be receiving calls! I can imagine her saying one day 'Hello Rector! Fancy seeing you here! Never expected it!' Who knows! But joking apart, there, in the presence of God, faith is completed, love is fulfilled, and joy is everlasting. Mary, we love you, we miss you enormously, we thank God for you and we thank God that now you are more fully alive even than you were here.

May God bless us all and, inspired by her example, may we go to live lives that are splendid, warm, open and simple. This we ask for Jesus' sake. Amen.

Some words at the start of a Remembrance Day service.

'I am conscious what a difficult day this is. There is a wide range of people here, from those who are very elderly to many very young children and everyone in-between. Some of us cannot remember the war. I was born right at the end of World War II. Some children have no understanding of what has happened in our country. Some of you remember it all too well; some of you fought, some of you lost loved ones. And there are some here who have sons fighting in present day conflicts, who live with daily tension and uncertainty.

Children, you're being really good and still, and in a moment you are going to be even better when we observe the two minute silence. But before that let's bring to God our own thoughts and memories and pray for forgiveness and fresh hope.

'Almighty and eternal God, from whose love in Christ we cannot be parted either by death or life, hear our prayers of thanksgiving for all those we remember this day, fulfil in them the purpose of your love and bring us all with them to your eternal joy, through Jesus Christ our Lord, Amen.'

4.Remembrance

It is of course the week of the humble poppy. At this time we become very aware of this beautiful little flower, and particularly this week it is in the news[1]. John Snow, Channel 4 news reader, will not wear a poppy publicly in his lapel because he does not wish to make a statement. By the same token he would like to remove the cross from around the neck of Fiona Bruce, the BBC news reader. With a logic which is as fragile as a snowflake, he feels that his own outrageously colourful ties are acceptable: they are not making a statement! And then there is Jonathan Bartlett, who is the convenor of a theological think-tank called Ekklesia, who feels that we should not wear red poppies because they make a link between war and redemption, so we should wear white poppies. This is post-modernism in full flow; a pluralism that will not nail its colours to the mast and a literalism that very often gets the wrong mast. Well, we are all wearing our red poppies this morning, and I want to suggest that they can help us to discover some theological truth about Remembrance Sunday. You may even like to take your poppy in your hand and look at it as I speak.

First of all, what we are doing today is remembering the **past**. We are remembering the two world wars. We are remembering the enormous loss of life. We are not remembering war as such, nor are we linking war to redemption, but we are thinking about the redemptive power of sacrifice as we remember those who laid down their lives that we might live. Therefore, we look back with enormous gratitude. Look at your red poppy and remember the blood that was shed, that we might have life and freedom! Then let that lead you to the greatest sacrifice of all, where on the cross Jesus laid down his life, that we might be free. In Hebrews 9.26 we read 'But now Christ has appeared once for all at the end of the ages to do away with sin by the sacrifice of himself'. The cross of our Lord Jesus Christ is the very hinge of history. In that moment on Golgotha, everything changed, as Christ poured out his life-blood for the redemption of the world; a redemption fully accomplished and yet to be universally realised. There in that moment, the power of sin, and of Satan, and of death, was finally broken; and things can never be the same again.

'Crown him with many crowns, the Lamb upon His throne.
Hark! How the heavenly anthem drowns all music but its own.
Awake, my soul, and sing of Him, who died for thee,
And hail Him as thy matchless King through all eternity.

Crown Him the Lord of peace, whose power a sceptre sways
From pole to pole, that wars may cease, and all be prayer
and praise...'
(M. Bridges & G. Thring 1871)

Look again at the poppy in your hand, and as you do so **look forward** to what one day will be. The poppy was not chosen because it was red. The poppy was chosen because it was a flower which grew prolifically in the fields of Flanders. And still grows, and forever will whilst there is life. The Flanders poppy speaks of life, ongoing, ever being renewed. So at the cross the red blood of the Son of God was shed, defeating the power of death and bringing life and immortality to light. And one day all things will be renewed in that new heaven and new earth in which righteousness will dwell. One day, 'all shall be well, and all shall be well, and all manner of things shall be well.[2]

Today is a sad day, a day of mixed emotion, a stirring of memory. Maybe years ago you lost a loved one; or maybe recently you have lost a friend, a husband, a wife, a brother, a sister. You have come to church and there is a sense of heaviness in your heart, and uncertainty about what has been and what is yet to be. Our second reading leads us to look beyond the present weariness of this broken world to that day when at the name of Jesus every knee shall bow. Listen, listen, listen! Listen to this again as you think about the sadness of war and the sadness of your own life.

> *I saw a new heaven and a new earth, for the first heaven and the first earth had passed away, and there was no longer any sea. I saw the Holy City, the new Jerusalem, coming down out of heaven from God, prepared as a bride beautifully dressed for her husband. And I heard a loud voice from the throne saying, 'Now the dwelling of God is with men, and he will live with them. They will be his people, and God himself will be with them and be their God. He will wipe every tear from their eyes. There will be no more death or mourning or crying or pain, for the old order of things has passed away.' (Rev 21.1-4)*

Do you believe it? Are you waiting for it? Do you know the logical conclusion of the death of Christ upon the cross is His reigning in glory where all creation will one day be gathered? There will be a new heaven and a new earth. Things will be re-constituted; all will be well; we shall understand; our tears shall be dried; our fears will be stilled; our sadness will be turned to joy, as together we stand redeemed in his presence. This is not whistling in the dark, it is living in the light.

But take your poppy once more, because between the cross and the new heaven and earth, between the inauguration of the kingdom and its consummation, there is a road and it is **the road of discipleship.** So Jesus said to his disciples 'Come, take up your cross!' The kingdom has been established, the power of death has been broken, and Satan has been ruined. But for the moment, this old world creaks on. The kingdom is now and yet to come.

So we inhabit a broken world. There is Iraq, there is Afghanistan, Israel and Palestine. There is random violence on the streets of Britain. There is global terrorism and there is global warming. I watched the news last night and two items sat side by side. First of all, the Remembrance service and all that was going on in London at the cenotaph. Then, in a report about the youth of Britain, an alarming statistic about the growth of sexually transmitted diseases was reported. We have, apparently, the worst record in Europe. The camera panned to a group of hapless university students, and they were asked 'Will your sexual habits change and will you rein in your emotions when you hear these statistics?' And they said 'Not a bit of it. Free condoms might help'. So we live in a fractured world. I was born in 1944, right at the end of the Second World War. My generation is the most blessed of generations. We have not seen war, we have not experienced suffering, we have not seen devastation, not close at hand. But do you know, we are also the most foolish, because we have taken that freedom and turned it into licence. We have moved relentlessly into endless consumerism, and we have delivered to the rising generation, my children and yours, a fragile and uncertain future. A generation that is technologically brilliant, but morally bankrupt, and spiritually desperately hungry.

Now it is into this situation that the call of Jesus comes to take up the cross and follow. To proclaim the great good news that the death of Christ has opened up a new world that is on its way to being delivered, and into which we can now enter. The good news of the gospel is that what God has accomplished in Christ, and what will finally be true at the end of the age, is flowing back into our own history, through the Church, which is the foretaste of the kingdom. So you and I this day, whatever our mood, are commissioned to go out into the world to proclaim the victory of the cross, and to invite people to enter into the freedom, the sanity and the joy of following Christ. We can do that with humility, and with grace, and with enormous confidence. We really can.

But that road of discipleship which is a road of victory and glory is also a road of suffering. Dietrich Bonhoeffer, the great German martyr who was senselessly killed right at the end of the war, on the 9th April 1945, said; 'When Jesus calls a man, he bids him come and die.'[3] You and I today, travelling the road of Christ, must bear wounds because we follow a wounded Lord, but we do so with hopefulness and with joy.

Oh Cross that liftest up my head,
I dare not ask to fly from thee;
I lay in dust life's glory dead,
and from the ground there blossoms **red**
life that shall endless be.
(George Matheson 1842-1906)

So keep wearing your poppy. It is one of 46 million, made for the occasion in a factory in Richmond where 42 people work throughout the year alongside another 90 people working in their homes elsewhere in the country. Wear it with humility, with joy, with pride. But wear it, most of all, knowing that one day the kingdoms of this world will become the Kingdom of our Lord and of his Christ, and He shall reign forever and ever and ever. To whom be ascribed, as is most justly due, all might, majesty, dominion and power, henceforth and forevermore. Amen.

1. Preached Remembrance Sunday 2007.
2. Julian of Norwich, 1343 – 1443. Revelations of Divine Love, ch.27.
3. Dietrich Bonhoeffer, The Cost of Discipleship, (SCM Press 2001) p.44.

Part 2

Reflection

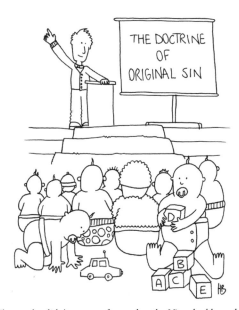

The creche didn't seem as focused as the Vicar had hoped

'When my son decided to give up on the Church, he said to me, "Father, that man (the preacher) is saying all the right things, but he isn't saying them to anybody. He doesn't know where I am and it would never occur to him to ask." '

(Bishop John V. Taylor)

Sermons on the subject of giving are not easy.

In fact they are so tricky that the temptation is to say something bland, or not to address the issue at all. But it needs addressing. If the local church does not set an annual financial target, money will always be a problem.

This sermon engages in a more expository manner with the text, in order to establish that there are clear biblical imperatives involved. The bit on tithing, and the simple suggestion that 50% of the tithe be directed to the local church, produced an enormous response. Although an obvious point, it seemed somehow to focus people's minds and cut through the complexities of their widespread charitable commitments.

Again, trust built up over the years is a great help. And in my case my well known financial ineptitude somehow enables me to be quite bold and direct. The church is full of people with tremendous financial expertise, who smile at my naivety, but respect my passion and directness. In sensitive areas, people need to be disarmed, but without any sense of manipulation.

I once heard the Bishop of London say that tricky situations need to be approached with a combination of charm and menace!

Worth remembering when preaching on this topic?

5.Giving is good for you

I am doing my very best to understand the economic turmoil which is engulfing us at the present moment.[1] I read my newspapers most days and I watch the news every day. I have talked to a number of people in St Saviour's who are very knowledgeable financially. I listen to Robert Peston, I know all about the United States tycoon Bernard Madoff who has made off with all our money and I understand something of the sadness that lies behind the headlines: the sadness of repossession, of debt, of unemployment. I shall never be an economist but I am a pastor and a sort of jobbing theologian and I know that beneath the headlines there are moral issues about greed, about expectation and longing, about hope and fear, and about human nature. The poet William Wordsworth said: 'The world is too much with us; late and soon, getting and spending, we lay waste our powers.' [2]

It is important to say all this at the start of a sermon designed to prepare us for our annual Commitment Day where we are looking for a 3.4% increase to maintain our ministry and mission over the next year.

Our text is 2 Corinthians 8 & 9, but particularly the first seven verses of chapter eight. The congregation at Corinth were very gifted but they were also very wayward. Just like St. Saviour's. No, only joking. about the last bit that is. Paul wrote a letter to them (1 Corinthians) and then visited. It was a painful visit because the church he loved was turning against him, as false apostles came in to challenge his authority. Paul retreated, wounded, angry and deeply troubled. The plan for a second visit was aborted and instead he wrote what is known as 'the severe letter' (now lost) which he sends to them by the hand of Titus. And then he waits. Eventually Titus returns and I can imagine him saying: 'Paul, do you want the good news or the bad news? The good news is that they have received your letter, they understand what you are saying and actually they are repentant. They are sorry. The bad news is that the false apostles are still churning things up, and still questioning your authority and reliability. But Paul, it's mainly good news.' So Paul sits down and writes 2 Corinthians and he is so excited and relieved and anxious and passionate and disturbed. He has so many issues he wants to address.

Now you and I, in that situation, would probably say: 'At this delicate point I won't talk about finance because it is always a difficult matter. I can leave that for another occasion.' Not Paul. Right at the heart of this letter he still comes back to the issue of money because it is on his heart. He has a project to raise funds for the church in Jerusalem, the mother church. So he says: 'I am not going to let go of this. In the midst of all that is happening I still want to talk to you about money.'

Now let me offer you five words. The first one is **motivation**. The motivation for giving is grace. The word grace is used five times in the opening verses of 2 Corinthians 8. The grace of God is fundamental. We exist by the grace of God, salvation comes by grace, eternal life is a gift of grace. Paul turns that theological word into a financial concept. He sees it through an economic lens, 'You know the grace of our Lord Jesus Christ, that though he was rich, yet for your sakes he became poor, so that you through his poverty might become rich.' (8:9)This incarnational passage is clothed in financial language. So Paul is saying to them, '*You have experienced the grace of God in salvation. I want you now to go on experiencing the grace of God through your financial commitment. It is through the releasing of things we possess that we experience afresh the grace of God and are enabled to pass on that grace to other people.'*

Paul is quite canny because he uses the example of the Macedonian churches up in the north of the country. There were churches at

Philippi, Thessalonica and Berea and their giving was magnificent. So Paul was saying to the people in the south: *'Just look how well they are doing in the north.'* (Some things never change! The north is always one step ahead!) *'They have received the grace of God and responded generously. Don't you want to do the same?'* Grace is not just about salvation, it's not just about feeling good, it's not just about being saved and going to heaven. It's about the way we respond. So the motivation of financial giving is grace.

The second word is **offering** because in verse five it says of the Macedonian churches that they first offered themselves to God and then to Paul's ministry. That is magnificent. Paul is saying to them, and to us, that financial response is rooted in a relationship with God through the grace of Christ. Giving is a scary, white-knuckle-ride journey, whereby we tell God this morning that everything we have and everything we possess belongs to him and we await his instructions about its use. Isn't that frightening? Isn't that wonderful? Most of the time I'm sure we act with integrity, but from time to time we need a reality check. 'God, I am doing all this with my money but actually it is yours. Am I on the right track?' And Commitment Day is simply a reality check about the level of my giving in the light of all that God has given to me.

The third word is **need**. Why do we release our money? We release it quite simply because there is need. Paul had been concerned throughout his ministry to raise a collection for the mother church in Jerusalem. This probably goes back to a reference in Galatians 2.10. He mentions it again in 1 Corinthians. A lot of Jewish Christians who had been pilgrims had arrived in Jerusalem and had stayed. Many of them were now widows and, as we know from the Acts of the Apostles, the relief of widows was an important issue (Acts 6.1). So Paul raises it again in this letter, urging the Corinthians to complete the collection that they began earlier for the relief of the saints in Jerusalem. What lies behind this financial appeal is nothing less than a call for the unity of the Church. He wants the church in Jerusalem, which is made up primarily of Jewish convert Christians, to understand that the Gentile Christians, out in the suburbs, were concerned for the mother church. They belonged together as part of one body. At the same time he wants the Gentiles to understand that their giving is a demonstration of that unity. They were in no way superior to the Jerusalem Christians, but part of the same family, 'all one in Christ Jesus.' It follows that our Commitment Day, which involves the release of money to meet need in Guildford, throughout our country and to the ends of the world, is at the same time a powerful sign of the unity and interdependence of God's people across all racial, social and economic boundaries. We do not live for ourselves or to ourselves, but for the mutual wellbeing of each other. It is a powerful message in a world so often given over to self- concern, greed and isolation. So that is why I am asking you to give, in order that money might be released as a sign of our unity and as a relief of the needs of the world.

The fourth thing that comes out of the passage is **eagerness**. Look again at the first four verses of 2 Corinthians 8. They are far more dramatic than perhaps we allow. 'And now, brothers, we want you to know about the grace that God has given to the Macedonian churches. Out of the most severe trial, their overflowing joy and their extreme poverty welled up in rich generosity. For I testify that they gave as much as they were able, and even beyond their ability. Entirely on their own they urgently pleaded with us for the privilege of sharing in this service to the saints.' Roll these incredible verses around your mind over lunchtime. This is radical giving. First, it is against the odds. They gave at a time of severe trial and intense poverty. We say to one another that we would love to give to God's work but actually it's a difficult time and we have got a lot on our plate just at the moment - now is not the time. That is not what the Macedonians said. They said: *'We are in a terrible situation but we are going to give joyfully in the midst of it.'*

So they gave beyond their means, but not foolishly. They said, *'We are going to give what we can rationally afford and we are going to give a bit more as well because it all belongs to God who is no one's debtor.'* Then they gave of their own account. There was no pressure. There were no sermons from the vicar. There was no arm-twisting, urging them to give to Jerusalem. Paul tells the Corinthians that the Macedonian churches simply wanted to do it. They decided they were going to do it and then they gave with a flourish. He says that they came to him to ask about the collection because they had the money ready and were eager to give it. Now when did someone last come to me and say: 'Vicar, Commitment Day is coming soon. I am really excited about it. How many weeks have I got to wait until Commitment Day?' I can never remember that happening! I've heard it said that the average local church suffers from psoriasis of the giver. It's a serious disease, in which the hand suddenly becomes frozen and immobile at the moment it is invited to reach for its purse or wallet. However this condition can be relieved by taking the patient out of the church, because it is clinically observable that it does not apply in the supermarket or in the restaurant or in the theatre. Isn't that interesting? Contrast the Macedonian churches with their radical eagerness.

At this point I want to say something about tithing. It's not there in the New Testament apart from one reference in the gospel where Jesus talks about the practice of the Pharisees. But in the Old Testament one tenth of whatever one possessed (and I think that in the Old Testament that would be gross and not net) was given back to the service of God. Christians down the ages have appropriated this principle as a bench-mark for their giving and I therefore want to challenge you about it. People say it is very embarrassing to ask for money, but I don't see why! I am quite relaxed. I know you have it and you know I know you have it. I just want you to release it, please. I simply want to ask. 'Do you give one tenth of your income to God's work?' I hope so because the more you give, the more you get back. That's not why you do it. But look at chapter 9 verse 6 (cf.Proverbs 11:24). The person who gives is enriched and the person who hoards becomes poverty-stricken. Isn't that fascinating! So don't be frightened about giving. But do be responsible. They gave out of what they could afford, not out of what they did not have (8:12). I am not asking for irresponsibility, but I am asking for a certain abandonment from myself and from you.

So tithing is a bold principle, elucidated in the Old Testament and assumed in the New, and I challenge you to do it. And then I want to suggest that, if you do tithe, one half of that tithe should be given to the ministry of St Saviour's, your local parish church. I am not saying that the whole tithe should be given, but half of it. You all have lots of charitable commitments in all sorts of places. I know that. I don't know all the details, obviously, but I am aware of your wonderful generosity. But I am urging that one half of your tithe be given to the ministry of St Saviour's, for two reasons. First of all out of gratitude for all the ministry we receive together in this place. Worship, teaching, pastoral care, hope, inspiration, opportunities for service – we have been given so much. But will you also tithe because you want to further that ministry, to see it grow in the days that lie ahead? You may feel I've been a bit tough but that's okay. We shall be taking communion in a moment and you can forgive me.

Here is my final point. Do you remember Barack Obama's brilliant campaign with its arresting mantra, '**Yes we can**'? I want to say to you as we face Commitment Day, 'Yes we can'. As we look at our needy world, as we contemplate all that we have been given, as we face a target of £955,000, we say 'yes we can!' Motivation, Offering, Need, Eagerness, Yes! Have you been following? You do realise that that spells MONEY?

Thirty-two years ago, in my first parish in the North West of England we had to raise money for a small building project. We wanted to take a few pews out of the back of the church to put in a meeting room. We wanted £2,500. It felt like a mountain to climb. They said, 'Vicar, that's enormous.' And I said, 'Yes.' And they worked at it, and I can remember the day my old warden, who was 85, who rejoiced in the wonderful name of Richard Baden-Powell Denton, came across my lawn and said: 'Vicar, about this money you want to raise. It's a lot of money. I was going to go away for a few days this year but I have decided not to bother and I have brought you my money.' And he gave me an envelope and inside was a £20 note. Yes, we can! We wanted £2,500 and we raised £5,600. We built the room without a faculty because I had forgotten about the legal requirements; we were visited by the authorities later, but it was too late and they decided not to prosecute. So if you want to see an illegal room in the Church of England, I can tell you where to look. It's still standing.

So we move from £2,500 to £955,000. Not a lot if you say it quickly. Thirty years have elapsed and everything has changed and nothing has changed. The grace of God has not changed. The love of God's people has not changed, the needs of the world have not changed and your response will not change.

1. The sermon was preached on 22nd February 2009.
2. W. Wordsworth, 'The World is too much with us'. (1807).

If preaching about money is hard, preaching about sex is harder, although the preacher is probably guaranteed a more attentive congregation.

This sermon was the third in a short series entitled 'Being Faithful.' The first addressed the issue of faithfulness within marriage, and the second was about homosexuality. There was a sense of curiosity about the sermons, some people saying that is was a brave plan, and at least one person saying that the subject of homosexuality shouldn't be addressed in a sermon.

Both sermons took the traditional line, that sexual intimacy is to be expressed solely within heterosexual marriage. The sermon on homosexuality was preached by a visiting gay man who tackled the subject with great integrity.

Within the 4 congregations that meet each Sunday there was much diversity of opinion (and one suspects practice) and whilst gratitude was expressed for our boldness, there were people who were disturbed.

So this third sermon was designed to offer pastoral wisdom, and insofar as it succeeded it was because of the long-developed relationship of trust between preacher and congregation.

A number of people suggested that some midweek seminars be arranged for deeper reflection.

6.Who will throw
the first stone?

Someone said to me yesterday afternoon, 'Will your sermon tomorrow morning be as riveting as the last two given by the other preachers?' No pressure then! Probably not, but the story that Claire just read to us from the gospel **is** utterly riveting (John 8.1-11). Jesus is teaching. A crowd gathers round him and suddenly there's a commotion and the teachers of the law drag through the crowd this woman, terrified, guilt-ridden, wanting to escape. They put her in front of Jesus and say *'Jesus, we have just caught her in the very act of adultery. Now you know, Jesus, the law of Moses says that she should be stoned. Jesus, what do you say?'* It was of course a trap. If he agreed with them then that would be very harsh and the common people who had been following him would begin to melt away. If he disagreed then it would confirm that he was a liberal teacher of the law and not, after all, one of them. For a moment Jesus doesn't say anything, then he bends down on the ground and begins to write with his finger in the dust and the tension rises. One of the teachers says *'Jesus, can you tell us what your judgement is?'* At which point Jesus straightens himself and he looks at them and says 'Which of you is without sin? You then must cast the first stone.' Then he bends down again and begins to write and as he does so, the accusers melt away into the crowd. The crowd thins out and suddenly there are just two people, Jesus and this broken tearful woman. Jesus looks straight at her and says 'Has no one accused you?' She says 'No one, sir.' Jesus says 'Neither do I. Go and leave your life of sin.'

This is a remarkable, intensely dramatic story and from it I want to try to draw out four things to help us pastorally at the end of this rather tense series. It's always a bit tense and exciting when you say you're going to talk about sex. I've noticed the numbers have increased somewhat in the last few weeks.

The first word I want to use is **framework**. The teachers come with a rule of Moses, a rule of the law. They say, 'This is what the law says' and Jesus upholds that. He actually gives permission for the stoning to start. This is a story of compassion, but within the framework of the upholding of truth. First, I want us together as God's family to understand that in all our discipleship including our sexuality there is a framework. That framework is the Word of God, written in scripture, incarnated in the life of Jesus Christ and illuminated by the Holy Spirit.

Last week Jonathan Berry, who is himself homosexual, came and talked to us and it was a very moving time as he drew our attention to Genesis chapter 2. God institutes marriage between one man and one woman; an institution publicly acknowledged, permanently binding, and the place within which sexual intimacy is expressed. The orthodox teaching of the church, and I believe of scripture, is that sexual intimacy is allowable only within the bond of heterosexual marriage. That is the framework. It is a framework laid down in Genesis and ratified by Jesus in Matthew chapter 19 and by Paul in Ephesians chapter 5. For many people it is a hard framework to hold but one to which I believe Scripture holds us.

The second word is **folly**. The folly of rash judgement that arises out of barren orthodoxy and blatant hypocrisy. For the teachers of the law, the woman is not a person so much as a moral debating point. She is a means by which Jesus can be trapped and their ecclesiastical power extended, and that, more than any sexual perversion, angers Jesus. Judgement must be made because there is a moral framework, but it can only be safely made from a position of utter consistency and moral integrity within the ones who make it. The only person qualified in this story to throw the stone is Jesus himself. This is a word for those of us who teach. I pray that when I teach, I will teach with clarity what I believe scripture says. But as I pastor you, my dear flock, pray for me that I may approach each particular situation with enormous caution and with all the compassion I can muster. To do anything else is utter folly. We must beware of the sort of moral rectitude which always makes truth seem black or white. Of course there are biblical absolutes but I have found that as, over the years, I try to be attentive to the Holy Spirit, my understanding has changed and developed. The truth doesn't change but my capacity to enter into its complexity has.

The third word is the word **forgiveness**. Forgiveness offered by Jesus. He upholds the Law of Moses but then he transforms it by refusing to apply the penalty. Here is the greatest miracle of John's Gospel. Jesus has turned water into wine, he's healed a dying boy, he's fed 5,000 people with a few sandwiches and he's walked on the water. Can there be anything more? Yes indeed! This one sentence: 'Neither do I condemn you.' Here is salvation for every person throughout all time. Jesus alone can say these words because of who He is and what he is about to do on the cross. 'He died that we might be forgiven. He died to make us good, that we may go at last to heaven saved by his precious blood.' So this is a story about forgiveness. 'Neither do I condemn you' says Jesus to the trembling woman.

Now we need to notice that the forgiveness in the story is both rejected and received. First of all it is rejected. Where was the man in the story? Nowhere to be seen at the critical moment. Just like a man. And what about the teachers? I'm fascinated by the finger in the dust because it is so insistent in the story. What is Jesus doing? Is he bored? Is he embarrassed? He may well be embarrassed by the crassness of these religious leaders. He may be embarrassed on behalf of the woman. But I like the idea, and I don't say it's anything more than speculation, that he is writing something in the sand that could be read, because the link between the writing and the disappearance of the accusers is very clear. So Jesus' finger moves in the sand and a woman's name appears and one of the teachers of the law thinks 'My goodness me, that was 40 years ago, I didn't think anyone knew.' And then a word, 'Ephesus' and another says 'The temple of Diana, no one saw me, how does he know?' This is fanciful but I like it! However, the real point is that at that moment they had the chance to receive forgiveness. They too were guilty. Not one single teacher of the law came and stood with the woman and said 'Jesus, I too need your forgiveness.' They went! They took themselves away from the source of light and forgiveness and hope and they drifted back into the dark claustrophobic shadows of their sinful lives. Is this a word for those of us who want to hide from the reality of what may be going on in our personal and in our sexual lives?

But if forgiveness can be rejected it can also be received – and here we come to the heart of the story. Two people stand together, alone, and Jesus' eyes pierce into the soul of the woman and he says to her 'My dear woman, has no one condemned you?' and she says 'No one, sir' and Jesus says 'Neither do I.' Jesus never says these compassionate things in a sentimental voice. There is a burning clarity about the compassion of Christ. He has a deep, deep love for the sinner and an intense hatred for the sin which has brought us so low.

In Revelation chapter 6 there's an arresting phrase about the 'wrath of the Lamb.' The concept is here in this story both when the teachers are condemned and when the woman is restored.

> *None other Lamb, none other Name,*
> *None other hope in Heav'n or earth or sea,*
> *None other hiding place from guilt and shame,*
> *None beside Thee!*
> *My faith burns low, my hope burns low;*

Only my heart's desire cries out in me
By the deep thunder of its want and woe,
Cries out to Thee,

Lord, Thou art Life though I be dead;
Love's fire Thou art, however cold I be:
Nor Heav'n have I, nor place to lay my head,
Nor home, but Thee.

(Christina Rossetti 1830-1894)

This is a word of liberating forgiveness for those of us who are willing to turn from our sin to a holy God to receive that endless mercy which 'droppeth like the gentle rain from heaven upon the place beneath' into your life and into mine.[1]

The final word is **faithfulness**. There is no condemnation of the woman but there is no condoning of the sin. 'Has no one accused you?' 'No one sir.' 'Neither do I.' Full stop. Close the Bible. Is that right? Not in my Bible. Listen! 'Go and leave your life of sin.' A new beginning. Ultimately this story is a story of cleansing. Many scholars think that the story is misplaced in the gospel and probably belongs in Luke. But for me it feels right here. For one thing the theme of the threat of stoning arises again at the end of the chapter (8.59) but also the incident follows John's recording of Jesus' words about the healing of the Holy Spirit which is like flowing water (7.37-9). Maybe Jesus is saying to the woman, *'I want you to know that healing, that forgiveness, that flow of the water of life about which I have been teaching.'* You see before you today a fairly tattered man but one who loves Jesus and longs to get it right. I too stand in need of cleansing and this morning together we can be ransomed, healed, restored, forgiven as the Holy Spirit pours the water of life into our lives.

Trebarwith Strand is one of our favourite Cornish holiday spots. There is a narrow road running down to a lovely stretch of beach.

I have stood there many a time and watched the water racing in to the narrow cove, covering all the debris on the beach and washing it out to sea. And as the tide recedes, all that is left is a vast stretch of clean smooth sand – ready for the next invasion of holiday-makers! Christ wants to move into our lives, clearing out all that is wrong, so that we can start again, fresh and clean.

> *O Christ, thou art within me like the sea,*
> *Filling me as a slowly rising tide.*
> *No rock or stone or sandbar may abide*
> *Safe from thy coming and undrowned in thee.*
>
> *Thou dost not break me by the might of storm,*
> *But with a calm upsurging from the deep*
> *Thou shuttest me in thy eternal keep*
> *Where is no ebb, for fullness is thy norm.*
> (Edith Lovejoy Pearce)

I pray that we may be filled afresh with the life-giving power of the Holy Spirit that we may stand ransomed, healed, restored and forgiven for time and for eternity. Amen.

1. Shakespeare, The Merchant of Venice IV. i. 182.

View from the Pew

Sermons – what do I hope for? First, I want to HEAR them. Even before I grew old and deaf, I marvelled that so many preachers speak to the front pews only, mumbling, or dropping their voice at the end of each sentence. An actor would never get away with this. We want to hear at the back of the church too. Perhaps every theological college should have an elocutionist-in-residence!

Having got rid of that grumble, what do I want to hear? Firstly, I want to be instructed. Not lectured, but instructed. I want the meaning and implications of a subject, usually based on a Scripture passage, to be teased out.
Next, I want to be involved. I want difficult bits, which have always puzzled me and which are usually avoided by preachers, to be aired honestly. If the preacher is puzzled too, then three cheers! I want him to think his thoughts aloud. If there are several possible interpretations, let's hear them all!

Then I want to be surprised. I want to experience the 'wow, yes,' moment, when a new insight floods me with delight. And I want to be entertained! I want the enthusiasm of the preacher to be infectious, so that his excitement at the subject makes me excited too.

I want to be focussed, probably by an anecdote or story which fixes the subject in my mind, so that when I think of the tale, I think of the sermon as well.
And finally, a little bit of levity never comes amiss. 'Lightness of weight, frivolity, unseasonable jocularity' (Oxford Concise Dictionary). Why not? Christianity is always serious, but never solemn.
Tall order? Not 'arf! So thanks be for preachers – especially the good ones I know and love!

Peter Snell

Early in 2008 we embarked on quite a long series of sermons entitled 'The Shape of Holiness in the 21st Century,'[1] based on passages from the book of Revelation.

We defined holy people as people who are heavenly minded, but at the same time deeply rooted in the events of this world. We tackled some basic issues of discipleship in a very practical way.

The ABC formula of these two sermons came about in a rather random way. We have two morning services each Sunday at which the same sermon is preached by the same preacher. On this occasion, me! I arrived at church to discover that the second service involved infant baptism, due to be conducted by one of my colleagues. The sermon as it was preached at the first service proved to be quite complex, and I realised that it would never do for an infant baptism service where the preacher needs to be sensitive to the fact that the congregation may contain unchurched people sitting in the front row, often feeling uncomfortable and bemused.

So the thirty minutes between the services was spent redesigning the sermon (No. 7). Reading it now, it feels quite conversational in tone, but I remember delivering it with some passion, wanting to connect with the visitors in church. I was not too concerned about the regulars – they could look after themselves!

It seemed to connect so I repeated the formula the following week. Whether it works is for you to decide!

7.Awake, Be Still, Connect

Sorry I got a bit confused during the baptism – old age and, possibly senility creeping on. But it was wonderful to baptise these two babies and to assure parents and godparents that we will do our part to grow them into a full realisation of the Faith into which they have just been baptised.

Over the last few weeks we have been trying to define what it means to be 'holy'. Not 'holier than thou', not 'holy Joes', not stained-glass-window saints with halos, but people who follow Jesus Christ and reflect something of his character in their daily lives. We have seen that to be holy is to be rooted in the world whilst visibly aware of another world where God is. To be holy is to be in Christ, in Guildford. This morning we are thinking about holiness and prayer, how a life of prayer is central to a life of holiness. So it's back to the strange, alluring book of Revelation and the first five verses of chapter 8.

John is on the Isle of Patmos, a sort of 1st century concentration camp, exiled by Rome because of the word of God. One morning as he prays he looks up and sees the heavens opened and God seated on his throne. Around the throne of God there are seven angels with trumpets and another angel with a great big bowl in his hands. People on earth are praying and the prayers are like clouds of incense drifting up to the throne. The angel puts these prayers into his bowl and sets fire to them. Then, as John watches, the angel upturns the bowl and the fire falls upon the earth. I'm not making this up, it's in chapter 8:1-5. Don't you just love Revelation! Such a strange book, but so exciting and colourful and dramatic. The question of course is 'What does it mean?' Well, let me try to answer that by giving you an ABC of prayer.

First, 'A' is for **Awake**. Tomorrow, when you wake up, I want you to awake to the fact that God is on the throne of the universe. There is a spiritual world. God is on his throne and waiting to hear from us. If you are not a believer and are not sure if God exists, but you would like to think He does, then can I invite you to experiment. Tomorrow morning, pray as though He is there, and see what happens. You may get a surprise! And for those of us convinced about God's reality, but too busy to pray – we too need a strong challenge. You know I wake up in the morning sometimes quite fearful. I am not an anxious person, but I am finding as I get older that I do wake up early in the morning and all the worries of the day flood into my mind. Particularly on a Sunday with sermons to preach. I have preached one, already this morning, this is my second and I am preaching a third one at Charterhouse School tonight. It can be stressful. (I know some of you wake up anxious because it's Sunday morning and you have to listen to a sermon, but that's another matter!) How foolish of me to say, 'I'm the Vicar, I know God is there, I am anxious about my sermon but I'll just go on being anxious'. What's the use of that? I ought to wake up and share my anxiety with God who is on the throne. It's not rocket science, is it?

Tomorrow morning you will wake up. You are worried about work, about the credit crunch, about the mortgage, maybe. You're worried about your teenagers - will any vestige of sanity ever impregnate their brains so that they become rational human beings? And if you're teenagers you wake up and wonder whether your parents will ever grow up and see sense. You have the dentist on Wednesday afternoon. You have to go to the hospital for the results of some tests. The firm has been making people redundant. So many things conspiring to unsettle us. But God is on the throne. Look at the passage again. There's a lot going on in heaven. Trumpet music (forget those twanging harps, trumpets are the instruments of heaven), angels worshipping, and this one angel clattering around with his bowl. God suddenly says, *'Turn the volume down. For half an hour I want to listen to what people are saying to me. I want to listen to what these people in Guildford are saying to me, I can hear David Bracewell, he is bothered about his sermon. He might well be! But I am going to help him.'* So wake up tomorrow and give God your worries and with them your whole life.

Then 'B' is for **Be still**. Be still before God. When you come to him, wait. If you are not used to praying to God you can maybe start with two minutes. Two minutes' silence. You can manage that, can't you? I heard the other day about a couple who were reaching their golden wedding anniversary. They were lying in bed and the wife said to the husband, 'How are we going to celebrate it?' He said, 'We'll begin with two minutes' silence.' Give God, tomorrow morning, two minutes. Before you put the kettle on, or maybe you want to do it over a cup of tea. Certainly before you go and get the post or bring in the milk or start looking at your diary. Give God a few moments. Be still and listen. He wants to talk to you, he really does. The Bishop of Oxford likens prayer to sunbathing.[2] To sunbathe you don't have to understand how the sun's rays work, you just have to go out there and sit in the sun. Woody Allen once said famously that 80% of life is about just turning up. Tomorrow, just turn up and give God a few moments. It is difficult because we live such hectic lives. We live under the tyranny of speed. We pack more and more activities into less and less time and we are not happy. The Bishop writes:

> We need to be detoxified from our busyness. We need to learn the secret that God walks at three miles an hour, the speed of love, the speed of the Spirit. No one says of a Beethoven symphony that if it were played 25% faster we could squeeze another piece into the concert. It has its own proper speed.[3]

God moves very slowly. He says, 'My child, just sit down for a moment'. It is no use saying: 'I want God's help but he's never around,' because God is saying: 'I would like to help you but **you** are never around'. Just be still before God.

Two questions arise. The first one is about God's existence. 'David, I hear what you say, but I don't think God is there. He's not listening. I have prayed many times and nothing seems to happen'. I have no easy answer to that question. All I can say to you is that I have followed God for fifty years now and sometimes he does hide himself but he always comes back. So sometimes you just have to hang on. Our old friend R. S. Thomas writes:

> *Prayers, like gravel flung at the sky's window,*
> *Hoping to attract the loved one's attention.*
> *I would have refrained long since*
> *But that, peering once through my locked fingers,*
> *I thought I detected the movement of a curtain.*[4]

A character in a novel of Anne Michaels, an old man, answering a question from his young companion, says 'Why do I believe in God? Because he keeps disappearing.'[5] Think back, have there not been moments when the curtains twitched and you knew the presence of God?

The second question is a bit of a trick question: 'If God knows all my needs, why should I bother praying?' Again there is no easy answer to that but I will tell you this. From time to time during the week my two-year-old granddaughter, Zoë, comes to our house. She is a real pickle and she usually wants to see Granny but if Granny is not there Grandpa will do. I know that one of the things she loves is those little round cheeses wrapped in that red waxy paper (Baby Bel, thank you Gordon!) I know she loves them and I have got a whole supply.

I am not too worried about her health, I just want her to like me! Her parents can sort out her cholesterol! So she comes into the kitchen and I'll say to her, 'What do you want Zoë?' Now I know what she wants, but I still say to her, 'Zoë, what do you want?' She'll say: 'Cheese, Grandpa!' I can't tell you what that does for me. It's just wonderful for this little girl to look at me and say 'Cheese, Grandpa'. I don't need to ask her the question but I do ask her because I want to hear her answer. Love delights to be asked for what it longs to give. God longs to pour his blessings upon you, but he waits for you to ask. He wants you to trust him and love him.

So A is for Awake, B is for Be still and C is for **Connect**. You wake up, you wait … and you connect, Talk to him. Tell him what you want to tell him: your fears, your hopes, your worries, your praise, your adoration. Anything goes, just tell him. Dr Johnson, in his travels around England, used to keep a diary. In the diary were his prayers to God. He prayed about his failing eyesight, he prayed about help in learning Italian, he prayed about his journeys, he prayed about his friendship with Boswell. Ordinary things. You may be angry with God and you need to say so. You may be grateful for something. You may need some help. Thank him for this service today and for the baptism of these children. Whatever it is, just connect, and as you connect with God he will help you to reconnect with your own life and the world around. Prayer is powerful. As we connect, so God works through us to bring change in his world. Remember I said at the beginning about fire coming down to the earth. When we pray, the prayers go up, and the angel with the bowl pours them back on earth, where fires are set alight. Christians are arsonists; they set fire to the world. They set fire to the bad things in the world to cleanse them and purify. Things change when we pray. The world is in a terrible state, there are wars and there is violence, but God is on the throne, and whilst he gives people the freedom to live without him, he is still in control and one day he will bring things together and all will be well. Heaven will be better than Surrey. Possibly even better than Yorkshire, though that's a bit more debatable.

Well, enough! Tomorrow morning, what are you going to do? The instruction is ABC. 'Awake', 'Be still' and 'Connect'.

1. The phrase is borrowed from David Smith's book 'Against the Stream: Christianity and Mission in an Age of Globalization.' (IVP 2003) ch.2.
2. In 'Prayer, A Christian Companion' ed. by Susan Hibbins, (Inspire 2006) p.5.
3. Ibid. p.7.
4. R.S. Thomas, 'Folk Tale' in Collected Poems 1945-1990, (Phoenix Giants 1993) p.517.
5. Anne Michaels, Fugitive Pieces (Bloomsbury Paperbacks 1998) p.107.

Visiting preachers were allowed
20 minutes

8.Faithful Witness

We have been looking at the question of practical holiness and last week I offered an 'ABC of Prayer' – Awake, Be still, Connect. I was worried that it was all a bit simple and that I would have insulted your intelligence. However a number of people said they found it helpful, so clearly your intelligence is not what I thought it was. I'm encouraged by that, so I want to do the ABC thing again tonight. But first we need the big context of the book of Revelation. What an astonishing book it is! The structure, as we have seen, is not linear – one thing after another building to a climax – but circular. Like a circular staircase where you climb higher and higher seeing the same thing from a different perspective.

After the well-known opening chapters, John has his vision of the throne of God (ch. 4,5). This is pivotal, and out of that vision the rest of the book unfolds. Chapters 6 and 7 describe the opening of seven seals. The seals are a panoramic view of the whole history of the world, from the point of view of the church, God's people. After the seals we have another sequence of seven trumpets (ch. 8,9).The trumpets give us a view of world history from the world's point of view.

The trumpet sequence describes God's judgements on the world, ending with his reign and rule being pronounced with the seventh trumpet. But, before the seventh trumpet is sounded, there is an interlude, a pause. That pause is chapters 10 and 11. Now- are you still with me? – this is what happens. First a glorious angel comes down from Heaven to the Earth. Expunge from your mind popular images of angels as overweight cherubs. This angel is magnificent, fiery and powerful. As he arrives a voice from Heaven says *'Do not sound the seventh trumpet, we do not want at this point any more of*

God's judgements.' So the angel comes down and he holds in his hand a small scroll for John to take, to eat and to digest.

Then there is a scene shift in chapter 11. John is invited to measure God's temple, the inner court but not the outer court. As he is doing so, two figures appear; they are called the Witnesses, and they have been appointed by God to bear witness to God's truth on the Earth. In verses 3-6, they speak with great power and effectiveness to the world. In verses 7-10 they are suddenly attacked and killed by a gruesome beast that comes up from the centre of the Earth. Finally, in verses 11 and 12, they are raised up from the dead and vindicated. Gordon, you are looking very puzzled. Stay with it. There are three things to be noted.

First of all, these chapters are about the Church's witness in and to a godless world. The scroll is God's revelation of His purposes in Christ. In chapters 4 and 5 that scroll is closed. Only Jesus Christ, the Lamb of God, is qualified to open it. It has now been opened and the purposes of God have been revealed to the world. The scroll is given to John, to digest and then proclaim. The two witnesses (6.11) represent Elijah and Moses, the Law and the Prophets. The proclamation from the scroll is a proclamation about the revelation of God's truth, the Law, and the application of that truth in daily life – the prophetic utterance. They are appointed to speak God's truth for a period of three and a half years, which is symbolic of a period of persecution (Daniel 12). And the truth of God will prevail (11.3,6). People listen, are afraid and respond. The church of Jesus Christ cannot finally be broken. That is the meaning of the measuring of the temple. Within that sacred space, God's people, gathered to worship, are safe and saved. But then they go out into the outer court and they become vulnerable, because that is the world where they are called to bear witness.

Secondly, as the witnesses speak they are attacked and apparently destroyed by the forces of evil. From time to time over the years the

Church is viciously attacked and is driven back. It is also a picture of what will happen in the end times when fierce persecution will come upon the people of God. 'Life is not made soft for Christians, though it is in the last resort made safe.'[1]

Thirdly, beyond that persecution (and it is a short time, three and half days as opposed to three and a half years), there is resurrection. The witnesses who have been destroyed, whose bodies have been laid dead in the street, are brought back to life again. Then the seventh trumpet is blown. 'The seventh angel sounded his trumpet and there were loud voices in Heaven which said "the kingdom of the world has become the kingdom of our Lord and of His Christ and He will reign for ever and ever." '

All that is background. It is a bit complicated and you might find it very strange. But just hold onto the central fact that the chapters are about the witness of the Church to the purposes of God in a broken and unbelieving world. Now against this strange and compelling background let me give you my ABC of Witness.

Witness is **Achievable**. Between the sixth and seventh trumpet of judgement, God says *'No, stop! I want to break into this sequence of judgement so that my servants can bear witness to an unbelieving world. This is my strategy.'* So in every age the church witnesses quietly, systematically, day by day by day to the Lordship of Christ. As the history of the world unfolds towards its seventh-trumpet conclusion you and I are called to bear faithful witness. Will you do it carefully with a certain reticence? The scroll is small; not everything is understood by John, or by us. Will you go carefully? Words are precise instruments, we need to watch our language. The Good News is not a puzzle, but it is certainly a mystery. A divine secret that Jesus reveals to those who lay themselves open to hear. Yet sometimes we speak of the Gospel as if it were a bargain basement offer, self-evidently beneficial and too good to miss. We need to be more circumspect. This is not a plea for hesitant, uncertain speech, nor a defence of confused speaking, but it is a recognition that our words more often need to be few, careful, and incisive. We need more haunting melodies, fewer battle marches.

So, tomorrow morning, I will not batter my neighbour into submission with many words, I will speak with care and with clarity and with reticence and I will leave the words as a bridge for the Spirit to do his work. I was speaking at Charterhouse Chapel last Sunday evening. At the end, the Headmaster spoke to me about Cary Gilbart-Smith, a member of St Saviour's, who was Senior Classics Master at Charterhouse for many years. He said, 'I want you to know that Cary kept the rumour of God alive in this school through very difficult times.' Careful words, seeds planted, that God will water in His own way.

When John is given the scroll from the powerful angel, he is asked to eat it, just as Ezekiel was in the Old Testament. And John says that it was like honey to his taste but bitter in his digestive system. The word we hold out is the word by which we have been redeemed and it is sweet and beautiful, it is precious to us. Therefore when it is proclaimed to people who reject it, there is for us a bitterness in its delivery. We have eaten the scroll, the Gospel is incarnated in our lives. So we don't offer an idea but ourselves redeemed in Christ. And rejection is hard – bitter. The eating of the scroll will be sweet and it will be bitter. So, my 'B' word is **bittersweet**. Maybe some of you have experienced the bitter-sweetness of proclaiming Christ in your place of work, or in your family? Some of you are here tonight and there are people back home who you love and who love you, who are thinking 'Whatever are they doing going to church on a Sunday evening? How sad! Is there nothing better to do than that?' And the thing that is beautiful to you turns to sadness because of their rejection. And if that is the case for you, I pray that God will give you hopefulness and courage as you continue to bear witness.

So, witness is achievable, it is bitter-sweet, and it is **cruciform**, it is the shape of a cross, and I mean that in three ways. The message that we proclaim is essentially the message of the cross. 'We preach,' says Paul, 'Christ crucified, a stumbling - block to the Jews, foolishness to the Greeks, but to those that are being saved the wisdom and the power of God.' (1 Cor 1.23) Tomorrow morning our witness is to Jesus Christ. There is no other gospel, there is no other person, there is no other answer, there is no other way. We preach Christ crucified. However you do it, your message is cruciform in the sense that the heart of it is a person, not an idea, not a philosophy, not a way of life, but a person, Jesus Christ crucified and risen.

The message is also cruciform because we proclaim it out of weakness. We come to our witnessing with a crucified, not a triumphalistic, mind. So the way we speak is cruciform. We come not in power, or in eloquence, not with manipulation, or pressure, but in humility, in reliance on the power of the Spirit, in hesitancy and in weakness. It is through that weak presentation – and by weak I do not mean ineffective or unthought-through – that the power of God is made strong. Finally, our proclamation is cruciform in the sense that we may well be crucified for it. This links back to the bitter-sweetness. We cannot expect necessarily that people will immediately respond; they may indeed persecute us for our holding to the truth. We may be derided, scoffed at, put down, ignored, thought of little account.

Finally, two words to hold on to. The first one is encouragement. We bear witness to Christ who already reigns over the church and the world. In the cross he has overcome the power of evil. Our task is to bear witness to that victory. We unveil what is hidden. We do not build the kingdom of God, we bear witness to its existence, as we lift the veil to show what we have been privileged to see: that Christ reigns on high and that one day 'at the name of Jesus every knee shall bow and every tongue confess that Jesus Christ is Lord.' (Phil.2.10,11) The challenge is to do it again and again and again.

I am due to retire in six or seven months time. What does the word retirement mean? I have no idea! But I am not going to stop preaching, not because I am a good guy, but because it is what I want to do with all my heart. And God will say to me and to Sue in our retirement 'do it again, do it again.'

> *We bear the torch that, flaming, fell from the hands of those*
> *Who gave their lives proclaiming that Jesus died and rose.*
> *Ours is the same commission, the same glad tiding ours;*
> *Fired by the same ambition, to Thee we yield our powers.*[2]

That wasn't the hymn I wanted to quote but it popped into my mind and it says what I want to say. Tonight we receive the flame and we bear it high day by day by day. It was Tennyson who said: *'How dull it is to pause, to make an end/ To rust unburnished, not to shine in use.'*[3]

And a Swedish Archbishop used to say to his clergy, 'Work yourselves to death, but slowly, please.'[4]

So, off you go. See you next week!

1. Evelyn Underhill, The School of Clarity, (Longman, Green & Co. 1948).
2. 'Facing a task unfinished' (v.3) Frank Houghton, (1931).
3. Tennyson, Ulysses, (1842) 1.6.
4. Bengt Sundkler, 'Nathan Soderbloom: His life and work' p.154, quoted in Donald Coggan, Sinews of Faith, (Hodder 1969) p.88.

View from the Pew

I remember my first Sunday at St Saviour's: I was a student at Surrey University, and shuffled in slowly with new friends, feeling slightly uncertain about the idea of finding 'the right church' for my student years.

I had been told that Guildford was a very well-to-do area where people spoke with a rather posh accent. Therefore, when the sermon came, I was a rather surprised to be addressed by a little northern fellow with a cheeky grin and a clear sense that Yorkshire was "God's own country".

In listening to David's sermons over the last nine years, there are three things which I have found make his style so rich and affable.

There are often moments during a sermon where David gets particularly passionate and seems to find a way to engage more fully with his listeners. Seemingly out of nowhere he shifts up a gear (or two), takes a stroll down the middle aisle of the church, and often addresses those in the front few rows by name, causing all to sit up and pay attention as special nuggets of truth, wisdom and challenge are imminent.

In my days as a student, my friend (now wife) Naomi was in Starbucks in Guildford town centre having a coffee with friends when in walked David, who was then taken aback to be noticed by three blonde nurses keen for him to join them. That Sunday, they all got a personal mention in the sermon and were delighted to be part of an illustration, and all three were touched by David's personable nature and often recalled that afternoon (and still do!)

Finally, I remember a specific sermon which for me was a great practical help in my own discipleship. It was on the subject of the word of God, its power to transform our lives and our responsibility to read, study and apply it to our lives.

I feel enormously privileged to have shared these years with David in the last chapter of his ministry at St Saviour's.

Matt Southcombe
Worship and Creative Arts Director, St Saviour's

I have tried to ensure that the 'View from the Pew' pieces reflect on sermons in general, not mine specifically. This one is the exception - a slight indulgence on my part, but the three points made encapsulate, in story form, the essence of good preaching. DB.

I preached a series of four sermons during Lent 2002 on four characters in the Passion narrative.

The sermons had quite a profound effect at the time: people were deeply moved and changed by what they heard. I had no sense, preparing the sermons, that this would be the case, and reading them again now I still cannot see why they were so effective.

At a human level it may be that character-studies always have a fascination, especially when – as in this case – they are linked to elemental moods and feelings. We looked at guilt, fear, identity and, in this sermon, isolation. When there is honest examination of these emotions in the light of Scripture, things often begin to stir.

From a divine perspective it may be just that God chooses from time to time to inhabit more deeply the words of the preacher for reasons best known to the Spirit. When that happens lives are changed. 'Not by might, nor by power, but by my Spirit says the Lord of hosts.'

This is the longest sermon in the book. You may want to break off in the middle to make a cup of tea – an option not available to the original hearers!

9.Coming Home

All of my life I have been an ecclesiastical ugly duckling! My family might say 'why add the word ecclesiastical?' but there we go! In the company of other clergymen I become incredibly tongue-tied. The prospect of going to Diocesan services fills me with horror. I invariably arrive at them late, dishevelled and very often wearing the wrong gear. A terrible thing happened to me at the Cathedral the other week: arriving late and scrabbling into my robes I hastily joined a procession, only to discover it was the wrong one. It consisted of a company of dignitaries and I had no right to be there. The vicar of Christ Church, and he's about six foot seven, appeared from nowhere and gently led me away! This sense of isolation, of being outside the circle, is quite funny but it can actually be rather painful. I have six more years to go before retirement, and I can only think the situation is going to get steadily worse! There seems to be no known cure.

Now tonight we return once again to the cross on which the Prince of Glory died. On these Sunday evenings we have been thinking together about the meaning of the cross. 'Oh teach me what it meaneth, the cross uplifted high' says an ancient hymn. We have noticed that the cross is both historic and contemporary. It is historic obviously in the sense that it happened in history. It was a decisive act. But it was also a completed act which makes it contemporary. Something was achieved on the cross; Calvary is the hinge of history. Everything was leading up to it, everything flows from it and nothing can ever be the same again. When Jesus died God's dealings with the whole human race changed. Not his love for us, that is unchanging, but the way that he deals with our sin and our rebellion in the light of the sacrifice of his Son. So the cross changes everything, because now in Christ we have become the righteousness of God. The cross is contemporary because

71

it was historic. Because everything changed then, we can enter that changed situation now by faith in Jesus Christ.

We looked also at our culture and we noticed that one way of describing this culture is to say that it is homesick. We have deep within us a sense of being exiles, of not being at home. Do you remember the four New Testament images of the atonement? One of them is the image of the family, rooted in the notion of reconciliation. The cross is the place where we are reconciled to God, where we are brought back home, where having been far away, having strayed, having gone into exile, having been lost we are found, we are brought back into the Father's house.

Now, we have tried on these Sunday evenings to give examples of what it means to come home to the cross. We looked at Simon Peter who was a radically insecure man, coming to Christ across the flickering charcoal fire, finding his way home, through the experience of forgiveness and restoration. Then we looked at Pontius Pilate and the issue of identity. Pilate, we saw, had the opportunity to break free from his identity crisis, by taking responsibility for his actions and following what he knew to be the truth.

Now tonight, we come to Judas Iscariot who betrayed Jesus Christ. Judas Iscariot who was radically isolated. A man isolated in heart and mind from Jesus, from the other disciples, from all that seemed to be going on around; a man whom Jesus is constantly seeking to bring out of isolation into communion, into new self-awareness.

Judas is mentioned fifteen times in the Bible, fourteen of them in the Gospels and one in the Acts of the Apostles. Each of the synoptics, Matthew, Mark and Luke, have him as a name in a list. There are a few more references, one at the end of John 6, then another where he approaches the Chief Priest with a proposal to betray Jesus. But there are four major incidents which help us thread together the meaning of his life. The first one is in John chapter 12 at Bethany, the home of Mary and Martha and Lazarus. Jesus is there and Mary suddenly, in an act of pure unadulterated adoration, pours out expensive ointment and washes his feet. In the shadows stands Judas. And Judas is angry at the waste of the money. It could, he said, have been given to the poor. And John adds 'He cared nothing for the poor because he was a thief and held the money'. And any money that goes on the feet of Jesus, by the same token, does not go into the pocket of Judas. That's our first major glimpse of him. And then secondly we see him at the last supper. Jesus has gathered his disciples around him and he washes their feet. Then he begins to talk about the one who would betray him and they all say 'What does he mean, is he talking about me?' Jesus confronts Judas: *'Come home, Judas, give up your betrayal Judas, sacrifice your plans'*. And Judas looks him straight in the eye and it's quite clear that he intends to go on to betray him and Jesus says 'What you do, do quickly'. He goes out, and John says 'and it was night'. Satan entered into him. The third incident is the moment when Judas comes ahead of the priests and scribes and soldiers to lead them to Jesus, and he betrays him with a kiss. Embracing his Lord and Master he kisses him into the arms of his enemies and onto the cross. Then finally in Matthew chapter 27 we have Judas filled with remorse, carrying in his hands the paltry bit of money that he's been given. He throws it down and it clatters across the floor of the temple - the priests do not want to know. They have betrayed Judas, as Judas has betrayed Jesus. He has done what they required, he has led them to Christ, and now they have no more use for him. And Judas goes out into the night – and hangs himself.

Peter denies Christ, Pilate abandons him, Judas betrays him. In the list of apostles he is referred to as 'Judas, who also betrayed him'. What led to that betrayal? Well, two things at least. First there was **greed**. It seems quite clear when you piece the story together that Judas had a great love of money, and it was at least in part that avarice, that desire to have and to hold, to get what he could for himself, that led him to the act of betrayal. Jesus had trusted him and made him the treasurer of the Apostolic band. He eventually goes to the High Priest and says 'What will you give me if I betray Jesus to you?' And they said 'We'll give you thirty pieces of silver', about five pounds. So for a five-pound note he was willing to give up his Lord and his Master. It was not an arbitrary sum. Thirty pieces of silver was the amount set in the Old Testament as the price of a slave. Do you catch the irony? In Philippians 2 we read that Jesus, being equal with God, did not think that equality was something to be grasped but made himself of no reputation and took upon himself the form of a slave. And Judas as it were underlines that divine condescension as he sells Jesus for the price of a slave.

Threaded through the motive of greed there is **anger**. Judas betrayed Jesus, but there was a sense in which Judas thought that Jesus had betrayed him. There seems some evidence that Judas was anxious to be part of a revolutionary and radical movement to overthrow the Romans. He was actually a southerner and all the other disciples were northerners, so he felt radically dislocated. There is a suggestion that he might have been related to Caiaphas and had infiltrated the band of disciples with the purpose of steering Jesus towards an earthly political messiahship which would give power and glory to the Jews, and in which Judas himself would be honoured. So the desire for wealth is matched by the desire for power and political gain. At the end of John chapter 6 we read that after the miraculous sign of the feeding of the five thousand the people gathered around Jesus, intent on making him a king. And it didn't happen, and Judas is mystified and angry. Just at the crucial moment Jesus goes off to the hills to pray. What an unpolitical thing to do! Then again on Palm Sunday the crowds cry 'Hosanna' - and Jesus turns away. At the root of these issues of greed and anger, there is isolation. This man was seriously detached from spiritual reality. He was obsessed with himself, his own concerns, his own well-being, his own material security, his own power, his own standing, his own reputation, his own career. Yet right through the story you can feel the warmth of the love of Christ saying to Judas *'Judas, Judas, come out of this wilderness of isolation, come out of this barren place of detachment, come into the light, sacrifice yourself for a greater cause. Judas, there is power in my weakness. There will be wealth untold in my eternal kingdom. Judas, come home.'*

So much for setting the scene – now comes the sermon! Hold tight, it won't take long. Two things. First, I want to put the issue of isolation into a cultural context. Our post-modern culture is one in which greed and anger have produced isolation. I think we are a generation seriously turned in upon ourselves. We certainly have a great love of money. 'Who wants to be a millionaire?' Our modern cathedrals are our shopping malls and we worship regularly at Tesco's, Sainsbury's and, if you're in a certain blessed company, Waitrose! We are a generation of whom it is said that we know the price of everything and the value of nothing. Because that is what the love of money does, it seriously skews our sense of values, our priorities, our understanding of what is right and wrong. We are the first generation to be defined not by what we produce, but by what we consume. And then there is anger. Many young people feel let down. They have inherited a world where so much was promised in the enlightenment dream: political freedom, moral rectitude, economic wealth, ecological security, yet the whole thing has begun to unravel. We do not know how long the planet we have abused will now last. We do not know whether our pensions will deliver, we have little job-security. We are morally confused about what is right and wrong to the extent that we have made clarity about moral absolutes the unpardonable sin. We do not trust our political leaders. All this has been delivered to this generation by my generation of foolish materialists. And the anger this generates sometimes comes out as violence and at other times as frivolity. In the light of its 2002 census, the youth culture magazine 'The Face' wrote:

'If identity crisis is a form of madness, then young Britain, 2002, is a schizoid manic-depressive with bomb-site self-esteem. Our status as the most boozed-up, drug-skewed, pregnancy-prone wasters in Europe is pretty much unchallenged.[1] Welcome to Christian England! Certainly our technologies have made us better connected, but we are more fragmented. We know more people, but we have fewer friends. We lead spider lives, we skitter along the threads of our world-wide webs picking up all kinds of delicacies, but we cannot find a place to rest or any source of genuine nourishment or intimacy. People today have a million different options to explore but no strong set of values to help choose which one might be best. So, the story of Judas, this story of greed and anger and isolation, is mirrored in our culture, and as disciples living in and being part of this culture we need to cultivate awareness so that we can live counter-culturally, bearing witness to the radical nature of the Kingdom of God.

But there is a personal dimension to the lesson of Judas. The isolation which is part of our culture is the isolation which is in the heart and mind of each one of us, a sense of being detached from what is real and spiritual and good and true. Maybe that is your story tonight. Let me say three things about such isolation. First of all it is **natural**. Sometimes we cannot help feeling isolated. I cannot help feeling isolated in a room full of clergymen. I don't know what to say. You find that astonishing, as you sit here Sunday by Sunday, that I could run out of words! It is a miracle for which you long and pray. But isolation is sometimes a defence mechanism for non-involvement. Some of us feel, temperamentally, outsiders. The human race is divided into observers and participants, and maybe you are an observer. There is nothing wrong with that, but if it leads to a sense of isolation, something needs to change. There is another aspect to this issue of detachment. It is possible for us to have allegiance, passionate allegiance, to the institution of the Church, whilst being radically disengaged from the person of Jesus. And that is the isolation which leads ultimately to betrayal. To those of you new to the Christian faith through your engagement in Alpha, I want to say, 'We need you, we need your passion, we need your freshness, we need you to be untainted by the experience of the institution.' Now of course you need the Church, there is no salvation outside the Church. But when our focus moves to the institution and away from the Christ, there is a radical detachment which leads to betrayal in the heart. I plead with myself, and I plead with you – get back to Jesus, even if it means cutting across the institution. Get back to Jesus, to his truth, to his life, to his priorities. Come home, where you'll be accepted and where you'll stand.

Here is the good news! Isolation is **curable**. You can come home. Judas at any point could have come out of his isolation and into the arms of Christ. Can I make that very clear? He was not the only one who betrayed Jesus. Jesus was betrayed by a whole network of people. By Pilate, by the disciples who ran away, by the High Priests who plotted, by the soldiers who wielded their instruments of death. So let us beware of castigating Judas as some sort of monster. He wasn't. He was an ordinary man whose heart had gone cold. Please do not listen to the theological nonsense which says that Judas was predestined to betray Jesus, that he had no choice. Do you really believe in a God who called Judas to follow him, knowing that he was simply trapping him because he needed someone to betray him? Do you believe in a Christ like that? It says in John 6:15 that Jesus knew who it was who was going to betray him. But the divine foreknowledge does not undercut human responsibility and freedom. At every point Judas was free to come out of his isolation, to come back, to come home. I've dealt with a very knotty theological problem dismissively in three minutes, and if you want to take it up with me further then come back at me, but I would want to stand by what I've said just now in shorthand form.

We need to note that the home-coming that I am urging is no easy option. It can be hard to come home, as the prodigal son found.

Radical Christian faith means committing ourselves without reserve to the crucified God. Following Christ does not create for us a cosy home and easy integration into our godless society. It makes us homeless and rootless and liberates us as we follow the man who had nowhere to lay his head. It is not a comfortable thing to follow the crucified God. We must bear wounds, for we follow a wounded Lord. So isolation is curable, but there is a price to pay.

But finally I want to say to you that if it is not cured, it is **deadly**. If it is not treated this coldness of heart will slay you. It is interesting to contrast Peter and Judas. Judas did come back. After the crucifixion he is suddenly filled with remorse, and he dashes to the house of Caiaphas clutching his 30 pieces of silver and the door closes in his face. He came back to the Priests and they turned their backs. But he did not come back to Jesus. Something had gone dead inside him. By contrast Simon Peter retained deep within him a love of Jesus, a desire to follow him. And it was that love that turned the remorse into repentance and renewal. With Judas it was not there. The love of himself was so hard and knotted at the core of his being that he didn't really have a love for Jesus, not really. So that when he is filled with remorse, there is an emptiness in his soul which cannot turn the remorse into repentance. That is the deadly thing. If we persist in being detached it may be that one day we will reach the place where we cannot make the response that we need to make to be made whole. This is what scripture calls the 'unpardonable sin', and if it worries you, then that is good, because it probably means you are not guilty of it. Because the unpardonable sin is the inability even to understand any more that Jesus is the way, the truth and the life. It is to look at the light of Christ and to regard it as darkness.

Oh dear. This is solemn stuff. Let me end on a positive note. Jesus never gives up on anyone, and he says right to the end 'Come home'. Last Monday morning I woke up slightly depressed, feeling a sense of futility and weariness, and I sat down early in the morning and I opened my Bible. Now I want to say to you I had not opened my Bible in a devotional way for ten days or more. And because I was feeling low, I opened my Bible. And I opened it at the page where I was required to open it by the scheme that I am using, but had abandoned. And the reading was Deuteronomy chapter 13 where God says 'I am putting before you my people a choice, between life and death – choose life!' And I thought 'Here I am, I've drifted away for ten days and on the day that I come back what do I find? Repent and be ashamed? No, no, no. Choose life, and you'll find me faithful'.

And so on the night that he was betrayed Jesus took bread and he broke it, and he said to Simon Peter 'Simon, this is my body given for you, take and eat'. And he says to Andrew, so full of love and evangelistic fervour, 'Andrew, this is my body given for you', and he says to Thomas, Thomas who was so brave, 'Thomas, this is my body given for you', and he comes to Nathaniel, 'Nathaniel, this is my body given for you', and he comes to Judas, and he doesn't hesitate, there is not a moment of hesitation, 'Judas, this is my body given for you. Judas, take and eat. *Judas, it is never too late to come home'.*

William Vanstone, in one of his Good Friday addresses,[2] tells of an experience he had as a parish priest in the North West of England. It concerned a young soldier Kenneth by name, 23, married with a young daughter, who in 1970 was invalided out of the Parachute Regiment with inoperable cancer. Kenneth's home was in Canon Vanstone's parish and by the time the Church became aware of his presence he was very ill indeed. Visiting him day after day and sitting by his bedside his visitors noted the agonising increase of pain as the time for his three-hourly injections of morphine drew near. Vanstone visited him on Palm Sunday and offered to leave a Palm Cross with him. Kenneth was unable to speak, so was asked to nod if he wanted the cross. He did not nod his head, but very slowly and painfully he raised both his hands towards the cross, took it, and slowly and with great care placed it in his pyjama pocket. After that, when each half-hour of agony began he would move his right hand slowly across his body and take hold of the cross.

The Canon called on the morning of Good Friday and spoke first to Kenneth's wife. 'We've had such a strange day,' she said. 'All this morning he was restless. I couldn't get him to settle. He kept moving his right hand as if he were trying to push something away. I was so worried because I couldn't make out what was troubling him. Then at last I realised that the nurse had changed his pyjamas this morning and she had forgotten to put the cross back into his pocket. I fetched it for him, and since then he's been ... well, you'll see for yourself how he is.' Vanstone climbed the stairs to the bedroom. Kenneth was lying perfectly still and peaceful with his right hand across his body, holding his cross. And so he remained until he died on the morning of Easter Monday.

'Now', said Bill Vanstone, 'I have no idea of the state of that man's soul, I have no idea what he thought of God, but I do know that the cross is powerful to penetrate into the most desperate situations'. Can I invite you tonight if you feel at all detached and isolated, to come back to the cross where Jesus died to set you free? It will cost you, it will cost you your life, it will cost you your money, it will cost you your ambitions, it will cost you your power – and it will give you the whole world.

> *Were the whole realm of nature mine*
> *That were an offering far too small:*
> *Love so amazing, so divine,*
> *Demands my soul, my life, my all.*
> *(Isaac Watts 1674-1748)*

1. Quotes taken from: 'Imagine, How we can reach the UK.' Mark Greene' The London Institute for Contemporary Christianity.
2. W. H. Vanstone, 'Seven Good Friday Addresses (2)' quoted in 'Darkness Yielding, Liturgies, Prayers and Reflections for Advent, Christmas, Holy Week & Easter' (Canterbury Press 2007) p.165.

As the sermon passed 15 minutes, fans of *The Archers* showed signs of panic

August is a quiet month – in theory.

Lots of people are coming and going, and there are quite a few visitors. Sunday worship feels more relaxed, with time and space to reflect. It makes one realise how pressurised normal church life can become.

For the last couple of years the sermons during August have tackled biblical themes through a biographical lens. So we have taken a specific Christian leader and spoken about their life and then opened up a reflection on the area of ministry with which they are associated. In this sermon the focus was on the Hebridean revival under the ministry of Duncan Campbell which led into a simple reflection on what Scripture says about revival.

Clearly the sermons cannot be exhaustive, but are meant to entice people to do their own reading around the person and the topic.

10.The Hebrides Revival

We have in our house a coffee-table book, 'Unforgettable places to see before you die.' Well there are about 40 places in that book and plenty of time for all of them before we die. Do I detect a certain mood of incredulity? One day, Sue and I want to travel by car up to the north of Scotland, take a boat 40 miles west to Stornaway on the Island of Lewis, and then drive 12 miles north until we come to the tiny village of Barvas. *'Barvas is one of the most desperate spots on God's earth, surrounded by monotonous peat moors and bogs, saturated by brine-soaked winds straight off the Atlantic and with as inhospitable a climate as you'll find in the UK, with a scattered community, with straggling houses along miles of open road.'* [1]

That is where Sue and I want to go before we die. Because in that very place, in the parish church in December 1946, God by his Holy Spirit came down in revival power upon that community. A revival which lasted from December 1946 until the middle of 1953. The people of Lewis are irredeemably religious, if I may put it that way. Most children, in the middle of the last century, imbibed theology with their mother's milk. Every Sunday was sacrosanct. Everybody went to church and most people went to the midweek prayer meeting. There have been various revivals in the islands over the years, one particularly strong one in 1939 just at the outbreak of war. And then the war intervened and many of the young men who had gone to war did not return, and there was a general decline in church attendance and a general sense of a loss of the presence of God on the island. But there were people there who were determined to pray that God would visit them again.

In April 1945 the parish of Barvas gained a new minister, a man called James Murray McKay who was a good and godly man. Shortly after his arrival he was summoned to visit two feisty old ladies living in a croft in Barvas. Their names were Peggy and Christine Smith and they summoned the minister to attend them. They said: 'Mr McKay,' (no first name familiarity in those days) 'we want to pray for revival. We sense that God wants to visit the island and our parish. Will you pray with us?' And he said 'Yes I will.' They said, 'We will pray in our cottage, three nights a week, from 10pm until 2am. Will you also commit to pray?' He said 'Yes I will.' And he gathered seven elders from the church and met in a barn in Barvas and prayed three nights a week whilst Peggy and Christine prayed in their croft. Peggy was 94 and blind, Christine was 92 and severely arthritic.

Later on in November, both the sisters in their cottage and the elders in their barn sensed on the very same morning that something was happening and that God was beginning to come to answer their prayers. They met together and Peggy told them not only that God was sending revival but that she believed that he had revealed to her the man through whom the revival would be led: the Rev Duncan Campbell. Now Duncan Campbell at that time was a famous evangelist, based in Edinburgh at the Faith Mission. So they wrote to him, and invited him to come in December to Barvas. Duncan Campbell was inclined to go, but the Faith Mission said in the light of his diary commitments a visit to Lewis was not possible in December. So he wrote back and said he could not come until the following Spring. When Peggy heard this she said, 'That is what the committee says, but God has told me that he is coming and he will be here within a fortnight.' Duncan Campbell, in his autobiography, says 'I cannot go into the details as to how it was necessary to cancel the convention I was going to. All I can say is that Peggy's prayer was answered and within a fortnight I was there.'

Just another word about Peggy. Later on when the revival was at it's height, she had another message from God that Duncan Campbell was to go to the most northern part of the island, where there was a lot of opposition to the revival, to preach there. Duncan disagreed, saying that he didn't feel any sense of God's calling to go up there, because there was too much work to do around Barvas. And then this:

> *Peggy turned her sightless eyes in the direction of my voice and her eyes seemed to penetrate my soul: 'Mr Campbell, if you were living as near to God as you ought to, he would reveal his secrets to you also.' Then she began to pray. 'Lord, you remember what you said to me this morning, that in this village in the north you are going to save seven men who are going to become pillars of the church. O Lord, I have given your message to Mr Campbell and it seems he's not prepared to receive it. Lord, give him wisdom, because he badly*
> *needs it.*

I'm glad there isn't a Peggy Smith in this church, or perhaps I should pray for a Peggy Smith!

But to return to the story: On the 7th of December Duncan Campbell arrived in Stornaway and made his way to Barvas and they had a meeting on that first evening. People gathered in the chapel and there was a lot of prayer and praise but nothing more. At the end of the meeting the session clerk said to Mr Campbell 'I feel that we should go and pray through the night.' Mr Campbell had just got off a boat, travelled twelve miles to Barvas, and conducted a meeting, but he went and this is what happened. The Deacon said: 'Do not be discouraged, Mr Campbell, God is coming. I hear the rumble of heaven's chariot-wheels.' And then Duncan said this,

> *God was beginning to move, the heavens were opening and we were there on our faces before God, 3 o'clock in the morning and God swept in. About a dozen men and women lay prostrate on the floor speechless. Something had happened. We knew that*

the forces of darkness were being driven back. We left the cottage at 3am to discover men and women seeking God. I walked along the country road and discovered three men on their faces crying to God for mercy. There was a light in every home, no-one seemed to think of sleep.

When Duncan and his friends gathered in church the next morning a stream of buses were coming from every part of the island and yet no-one could find out who had told them to come. The Spirit of God was at work. All over the church men and women were crying for mercy. Some fell into a trance, some swooned, many wept. Campbell pronounced the benediction and almost all left the chapel. Suddenly a young man started to pray. He was so burdened for the souls of his friends that he prayed for almost three quarters of an hour. During this time the people returned to the church, joined by many others, until there were twice as many outside the church as inside. In some amazing way the people gathered from Stornaway and Ness and different parishes. It was 4am the following morning before Duncan pronounced the benediction for a second time. That is how the revival began in 1949, on the 8th of December, in the parish of Barvas, on the island of Lewis, and that is why Sue and I want to go and visit it. You may wonder if there is any point so many years on. All I know is that this story has been with me for years and I want to go.

Let's leave the history for a moment and ask this basic question: 'What brings revival to the church at any time?' The answer, unequivocally, is God. God alone can revive the church and the nation. God alone can bring revival. However, God is really rather good at co-operating with weak human beings, and the revival that God brings is very often directly related to the preparation that the people of God make. And right at the heart of that preparation is the ministry of prayer. Through the summer of 1949 James Murray Mackay used to say to his wife, 'It will only take a spark, it will only take a spark for God to come down.' We read in Hosea 10 .12, 'Break up the unploughed ground, it is time to seek the Lord until he comes.' The Psalmist says, 'Will you not revive us again that your people may rejoice.' And in the Island of Lewis and in the parish of Barvas they prayed. Someone has written,

> *Why have these places been so favoured, why has the Lord been pleased to shower his blessings and reveal his presence in these remote parts?' Why? Because they prayed. They prayed expectantly, they prayed persistently, they prayed with awesome passion, they prayed believingly. They learned to pray as they prayed. The Holy Spirit has taught them in their praying. They have learnt the secret of pressing through into the court room of heaven and touching the throne. They have waited upon God.*

Mary McCloud, a lady who lived in Barvas, said of the Christian community there: 'It was a community of prayer. Though the secret of God visiting the earth again through his church in revival power may be attributed to many things, right at the heart of the many things lies a praying community.'

In conclusion I want to draw our attention to that famous passage on revival in 2 Chronicles 7. The temple that Solomon has built for the glory of God is ready to be dedicated, and one night God appears to him: 'I have heard your prayer and have chosen this place for myself ... when I shut up the heavens so that there is no rain, or command locusts to devour the land, or send a plague among my people ...' Why would God do that? Why does it feel that He's doing that now in Britain? Why is our own culture so barren and joyless? Is it the credit crunch? Is it the housing market? Is it the inflation rates? No, no, no. It is because God has shut the heavens on a godless generation.

And he is looking for a people who will pray that the heavens may be opened. That is the theological reality behind our cultural distress. The politicians may know a lot but they don't know everything. By a long chalk! And of course the same is true of the Church. Our dear Church of England is in a parlous state, is it not? So what is the challenge? The challenge is that when these things are the case, when there is barrenness, when there is drought, then ' If my people who are called by my name will humble themselves, and pray and seek my face and turn from their wicked ways, then will I hear...' What is the solution to barrenness? What is the challenge for revival? It is that the people of God cry out to God for him to come. The state of the nation lies at the door of the church. Will we do anything? Or will we not?

We are to do three things. We are to **humble ourselves** before God. We are to look to God to bring change, to bring refreshment, to bring renewal and to bring revival. We must humble ourselves before God. We cannot engineer revival, we can only plough up the ground. Listen to this.

> *'Barvas is a golden star, one of the choice companies battling for the kingdom. Yet Barvas has no organ, no guitars, no orchestra, no choir, no hymnal even; we could add that there are no organisations, no coffee mornings, no children's programmes, no church staff, no seminars, no highly prized programmes. Apart from the Sunday services it has the weekly prayer meeting, that's all.'*

Now the writer goes on to say that churches at different times will need all these things, of course they will. But the issue is that we can be so occupied with the trappings, when God is simply waiting for the worship and adoration of our hearts. He is waiting for us to get to the place where he can put within us something of the burden he bears for a lost humanity which would then drive us to our knees to intercede mightily in the power of the Holy Spirit.

In Barvas they prayed. We have our ecclesiastical structures and patterns of leadership and Barvas prays. We have our coffee mornings, our social events and bright ideas and Barvas prays.

It is a process of stripping down and humbling ourselves to say that he only can bring about the change we want to see, so that the rain may water the earth as it is doing physically tonight, that fruit and growth and life and joy may sprout up in a broken world.

Then we must **pray and seek God's face**. We pray with intent when we seek God's face. You have a loved one, and they have gone away, maybe migrated to Australia, and they are returning home for a visit. It's a year since you saw them and you park the car at Heathrow and make your way to the arrivals area. You look anxiously at the screens, 'Expected...landed...in baggage hall.' And you stand with the hordes behind the barriers. What are you doing? Are you looking around casually? Are you saying any face will do? No, no. You are seeking with all the intensity of your heart for one face, a particular face, a specific face, for the face that no other face will replace, for the face of your loved one that you haven't seen for a year. And as the people come through you scan and you search and you will not be distracted until the moment when you see, face to face, and you embrace and life is complete again. 'If my people who are called by my name will humble themselves and pray and seek my face.'

And then, thirdly, we must **turn from our wicked ways**. When the seven men praying in the barn in the winter of 1946 met on one particular night, kneeling in the straw and pleading with Almighty God, a young deacon from the Free Church stood up and read Psalm 24: 'Who shall ascend the hill of the Lord, who shall stand in his holy place? He that has clean hands and a pure heart, who has not lifted up his soul to vanity nor sworn to deceive his neighbour.' He read the passage again and then he challenged the praying group. *'Brethren' he said 'we have been praying for weeks, waiting on God, but I would like to ask now are our hands clean? Is my heart pure?'* As they continued to wait before God, his awesome presence swept into the barn. At four in the morning, in the words of Duncan Campbell, *'they moved out of the world of the common and the natural, into the sphere of the supernatural.'*

So the cost of revival is the cost of prayer, which is humble and purposeful and repentant, and when that happens God comes down. One of the most dramatic events happened in a place called Arnol just north of Barvas. Duncan Campbell recalls it and he says that one night they were praying in a cottage through the night and he felt it on his heart to ask the man next to him, who was a blacksmith, to pray. And this big, burly blacksmith called John Smith stood up and he prayed, and he challenged God. He said *'God, you are a covenant-keeping God, I'm challenging you tonight to keep your promise. You said that you would come.'* Duncan Campbell said that he had never heard anything like it and that at that moment the whole cottage shook, the cups and saucers on the dresser shook and some people who had gone to sleep on the stairs were woken. The cottage shook. Duncan Campbell was not a dramatic person, he was a dour Scotsman. I had the privilege of hearing him preach in Leeds in 1964. I was just a student but was held spellbound for an hour and a quarter as he preached on revival: I remember it so well. And if Duncan Campbell said the cottage shook, then the cottage shook.

So there you have it. Prayer and revival, the Smith sisters, the prayer that humbles us before God, as we bring to him the desires of our hearts for Church and Nation. Prayer that is focussed upon his face, that turns away from all that is wrong and opens us in purity to the coming of God.

God has brought revival many times in history. I don't think we've seen it in the British Isles since 1904 in Wales and the 1950s in the Hebrides. Can he do it again? Yes, of course. He will do it again when he finds a church he can trust and when he finds a people whom he can trust. God found such a people in Lewis. Could we be such a people?

Let us pray.

God our Father, I pray that you will trust us and that we may trust you. Lord, I'm preaching about things of which I have little understanding, preaching quite beyond the realm of my experience. But, Lord, I've been fascinated for years by revival. Lord I thank you for the tiny, tiny touch of your renewing Spirit that we experienced at one point in the history of this church which changed everything in a moment of time and that was just the slightest movement of the curtain separating heaven and earth. Lord, I can't imagine what would happen if you flung the curtain wide for a moment. We live, Lord, in the gloom of half-hearted commitment. We live in the twilight of uncertain spirituality. We are clogged by materialism, by fear, by anxiety, and by a deep lack of understanding of your word and a persistent failure to wait upon your Spirit. And, Lord, I sense that if together as a congregation we were to go deeper and wait longer there is no telling what you would do. We might become a church that you would trust. Lord, we pray that you would come amongst us by your Spirit, that you would touch our lives afresh with your Spirit, for your mercy's sake. Amen.

1. It would be cumbersome to provide detailed footnotes for all the various incidents I have quoted in the sermon but I am listing the main sources from which they are drawn.
Duncan Campbell, 'The Price and Power of Revival, Lessons from the Hebrides Awakening' (The Faith Mission, 1956)
Arthur Wallis, 'Rain from Heaven' (Hodder and Stoughton 1979)
Colin Whittaker, 'Great Revivals' (Collins 1990)
Colin and Mary Peckham, 'Sounds from Heaven The Revival on the Isle of Lewis 1949-1952' (Christian Focus 2004)

View from the Pew

If I am honest, I genuinely look forward to the sermon. I anticipate it to be another opportunity to learn from someone who has put aside their time to discover what God has to say for my week ahead. I hope each sermon will be a life-changing experience in the sense that change is usually achieved by small steps. I want to see God a little more clearly today than I did last week, I want to take away one point or quotation that will help me live a more Spirit-filled life when I re-enter my normal world tomorrow.

I don't really need beautifully crafted words or cleverly worked amusing stories to engage in this lopsided dialogue, although style can be uplifting and entertaining. A lecture could give me researched facts and polished argument, a seminar might give me the opportunity to interact and spark ideas: good things, but not what I want from a sermon. I want truth and passion, truth derived from experience converted into passion to inspire.

If the sermon relies heavily on personality or fashion to succeed I have many excuses to switch off, to reject the concepts explored. When the sermon demonstrates personal learning and revelation, whatever its presentation I ignore it at my loss.

Here is the difficult thing; I have enormous expectations of the sermon-giver. I am looking for the integrity of a living relationship with God so that I can in turn examine my own experience. I want to test my own understanding and growth by filtering the sermon to make my personal response. I need space and time to do this; I might need days, or months, depending on the magnitude of the lesson I have learned.

Pulpit to pew a dialogue? Yes indeed but one of mutual dependency and willingness to learn.

Marion Peters

This sermon has a rather odd history.

I wrote it on holiday, ready to preach on the Sunday I returned home. Ahead was a series on the Epistle to the Ephesians and this was conceived as a rather homely curtain-raiser to a challenging book.

But we have a lot of preachers at St Saviour's, the rotas are complex, I am getting old... and to cut a long story short someone else was down to preach. However, having worked on it, I tried it out on a group of cancer patients who meet once a month at Loseley House, a stately home just outside Guildford. They were really appreciative, and it led to a creative discussion about the value of friendship, so I decided to include it.

It's hardly a theological heavyweight discourse (not that many of my sermons are!) but it seemed to resonate quite deeply.

11.Friends

I hope you've had a good week. By my standards, where a trip into Woking is quite an event, mine has been quite exotic. I would like, if I may, to tell you about it in a moment. But first, a verse from Ephesians:

> *I have heard of your faith in the Lord Jesus and your love towards all the saints, and for this reason I do not cease to give thanks for you as I remember you in all my prayers. (1.15)*

Ephesians, as we are discovering in this current series of studies, is a magnificent epistle, providing, as it does, a panoramic view of human history. God is at work to reconcile the whole creation to himself through the death, resurrection and exaltation of Jesus, and the calling of the Church is to make this visible to a watching world. If that doesn't sweep away your worries about the timing of your Sunday lunch I don't know what will. But Paul always has his feet on the ground, and in this verse he shows a very human desire to acknowledge the faith and love of the believers in Ephesus. He may not have known them all personally (in the same way that he knew the Christians at Corinth) but he knew about them, and they knew about him (1.15, 3.2), and he feels a bond of love and an urge to pray. Paul was a missionary statesman, a first-class theologian and an apologist for the Faith, but let's never forget that he was also, a loving pastor caring for his people, grateful for their friendship.

So back to my exotic week! It began with a phone call late on Sunday evening from Alex, one of my godsons, to tell me that his father (aged 89) was dying in a Bristol hospital. Derek David Whitfield Mowbray was the man who helped me to crystallise my faith in Christ, nurtured me in discerning my call to ordination, employed me as his organist in the church where he was vicar in Leeds, and showered me with care and wisdom, in conversation and by letter (an average of one a week over a period of two years, beautifully hand-written and arriving on a Monday morning). I only ever referred to him as Dr. Mowbray (he has five theological degrees!) and as I knelt by his bedside, helping him to drink through a straw at the instruction of the nurse, and stroking his hand, I thanked God from the bottom of my heart for this good and godly mentor. I owe him my life.[1]

From Bristol Sue and I resumed the journey we were due to make that day to the Lake District. We had arranged to stay for a few days with a much loved friend, Jean Filkin, at her home in Windermere. Jean was my landlady when I began my ministry as a raw curate in Tonbridge, Kent, and we have remained firm friends for over forty years. More than anyone I have ever met, Jean has the gift of hospitality, and Sue and I visit her whenever we can. In fact we have to remember to book early to avoid disappointment because she has a regular flow of visitors. She lives not in a neatly kept house, but in a wonderfully relaxed home, full of dogs, music, books, conversation and laughter. She is a delightfully accomplished pianist and a stunning cook. So we sit around, stroking dogs, listening to music, and reading books and newspapers, whilst Jean potters around her slightly chaotic kitchen – and then suddenly an incredible, mouth-watering meal appears. It is a great place to be, and she is a special friend.

Whilst staying there I spent a couple of hours with a local Vicar, Tim Montgomery. He and his wife Sue are leading a thriving church in Cumbria which is developing a resource ministry for churches across the Carlisle Diocese. We talked long and hard about things pertaining to church leadership: I shared with him my hopes and fears about 'retirement' and he reflected on the next phase of his own work. Two colleagues giving mutual support and encouragement over a cup of coffee, and later, with our wives, over a bottle of wine!

The next day I left Sue in Windermere and took a train to Portsmouth to attend the farewell service for Bishop Kenneth Stevenson who is retiring as Bishop of Portsmouth because of ill health. The Cathedral was packed. Kenneth preached from Psalm 85 about mercy and truth, the twin attributes of a fruitful Christian community, and celebrated Communion. Then there were speeches and presentations to him and his wife Sarah as they took their leave of the Diocese. It was very moving, and as I sat there I reflected on the relationship Kenneth and I had built whilst he was Rector of Holy Trinity, Guildford. From very different traditions, and widely differing capabilities (I a minnow to his immense theological scholarship and liturgical expertise), we forged a relationship which enabled us to cross ecclesiastical boundaries. What we did share was a mutual disrespect for the pomposities that often disfigure the face of the church. Sitting at the back of the Cathedral I thanked God for his forthright ministry, and the remarkable courage he has displayed during the years of his debilitating illness.

So that was my week. Thank you for listening to this rather self-indulgent ramble. But here is the point. Relationships are the stuff of life, the glue which holds together the whole fabric of our frenzied activity. Mentor, friend, colleague, Bishop. Dr. Mowbray, Jean, Tim, Kenneth....I do not cease to give thanks for you, remembering you (but not as often as I should) in my prayers.

So here are three points to ponder. First, **all friendships are to be treasured**, but those rooted in a common Christian faith are beyond price. Where two people meet together in Christ there is unity, a common bond of gratitude for the grace in which we stand, an absence of pretence or rivalry, a shared hope and purpose. Pray that our relationships here will be gracious and loving. Pray that we may grow an inclusive community. Pray for the gift of hospitality. People exploring Church are not looking for fellowship (a terrifying concept) or friendship even. They want to make friends.

Then, friendship is a sign of Kingdom life in a fast-moving, uncertain culture where quality relationships are often replaced by casual contacts, and people feel isolated. In the business world you swiftly surf your networks to gain what you can; in the real world you slowly build your friendships to share who you are. Our frenetic culture, distorted by fear, ambition and greed, desperately needs to be exposed to quality, self-giving relationships. Make your home a place of rich hospitality where others can relax and be refreshed. 'An Englishman's home is his castle' is one of our saddest proverbs. By contrast the marriage service talks about the new couple making their home 'an image of (God's) eternal kingdom.'

Finally, **keep your friendships in good repair.** The phone call from Alex brought me a stab of guilt. I had not contacted Dr. Mowbray for a very long time. I felt a sad chastening when his face lit up with pleasure on seeing me, and when he asked me to come again. We have no excuse not to keep in touch in our communication-obsessed society: telephone, mobile, e-mail, text, Facebook, Twitter... And as a technological dinosaur, can I put in a plea for the good old letter? There is nothing quite like receiving a real letter, handwritten, with a stamp and delivered by a real postman. I can see the mouths of those under thirty dropping open in incredulity. So be it! And of course, undergirding all this, the desire to pray for those we know and love. Keep a list, and pray systematically for your friends.

Towards the end of his life, Paul is in prison for the final time. He has fought the fight, he has kept the Faith, and now he awaits the moment when he will be with Christ, 'which is far better.' (2 Timothy 4.7, Phil. 1.23) But even now, friendship fills his mind. He writes to the young Timothy, who has been a son in the Faith to him, 'Do your best to come to me soon...Get Mark and bring him with you...When you come bring the cloak that I left with Carpus at Troas, also the books and, above all, the parchments.' (2 Tim. 4.9-13) At the end of his life, the greatest theologian the world has ever seen simply wants a coat, some books, and most of all, two friends.

My week past has been bounded by seeing four friends, two of them struggling with serious illness. Such encounters, especially when there is sickness, bring a sense of perspective. What are the things that matter most in our bustling lives? The writer to the Hebrews talks about removing things that can be shaken so that what cannot be shaken can remain. (Heb. 12.26-28) It conjures up for me the picture of a giant sieve, shaken from side to side, separating out what is not needed, and leaving safe and secure the things that really matter. So what can be shaken? Your boss's targets? Your Vicar's latest bright idea to grow the church? Your efforts to secure promotion, my ambitions to be invited to speak on a prestigious platform? Yes, all this and much more. These things may not be inconsequential but if the sieve really gets shaken, through illness, through unexpected tragedy, through a new vision of the glory of God, they will not remain. So what will? What, in extremis, would you want to have and hold? The answer I would suggest is: 'My faith and my friendships.' Without these, all we strive for at a material level is of little worth. With these in place we can be utterly relaxed about the rest of life.

'Dr. Mowbray, Jean, Tim, Bishop Kenneth' (and each of us of course will add our own names) 'I do not cease to give thanks for you as I remember you in my prayers.'

1. Between preaching this sermon and it being published, Dr Mowbray died. On Saturday 10th Oct 2009 just before his 90th birthday he passed into the presence of his Lord.

This is not really a sermon.

It was one of three short talks given at the end of evening services during Autumn 2009.

I was reflecting on some of the themes that have become important to me over forty years of ministry. What is written here is a distillation of what I spoke about in that very informal setting.

Quite a few people stayed to listen and participate in what had been billed, rather grandly, as a seminar. There was time at the end for questions - and there was no shortage of contributions!

I was conscious that in the audience there were quite a few people who were eminent leaders in their own field, and it was interesting to reflect on where Church leadership and secular leadership overlap, as well as the points at which they diverge.

12.Leadership

I was ordained on Trinity Sunday 1969 in Rochester Cathedral by the then tallest Bishop in the Church of England, Dr David Say. He was 6' 6" – and when you add a mitre near enough 7'! So this year (2009) marks forty years of being ordained.

During that time I have worked in four locations: Tonbridge, Shipley (West Yorkshire), Bolton and Guildford. Before ordination my preparation involved three years at university, one year working in a Parks and Cemetery Dept. and two years at theological college. So when you add those six years to six years of being a Curate I had twelve years of training for Christian leadership. I was exhausted before I started!

However it is only in the last ten years that a number of experiences have encouraged me to reflect on what it means to be a leader in the Church of God. First of all I became involved in the 'Leaders of Larger Churches' network, helping to run conferences and workshops for people leading churches of 350 or more members. This experience has filled me with hope for the future of the church. I have met many dedicated, passionate, imaginative men and women devoted to growing the local church. Then I was invited to lecture in Pastoral Studies one day a week at a leading Anglican theological college. I did it for two years and found it wonderfully stimulating and enormously frustrating. The frustration came from the feeling that my students were driven at a frenetic pace by an agenda designed to stimulate their minds but not necessarily to feed their souls. I encountered a good deal of quiet despair. Whilst working there I read Henri Nouwen's book on leadership in which he says:

Thinking about the future of Christian leadership, I am convinced that it needs to be a theological leadership...This cannot be just an intellectual training. It requires a deep spiritual formation involving the whole person – body, mind and heart. I think we are only half aware of how secular even theological schools have become. Formation in the mind of Christ, who did not cling to power but emptied himself, taking the form of a slave, is not what most seminaries are about. Everything in our competitive and ambitious world militates against it. But to the degree that such formation is being sought for and realized, there is hope for the Church of the next century.[1]

My third experience has been the opportunity to mentor individual Church leaders desperate enough to beat a path to my door. Currently I am seeing six and I am finding it an enormous privilege. I am grateful to God for the sheer quality of the people he is raising up and calling into ordained ministry. But whilst being excited I am also troubled by the great need there is for the nurture of leaders who are perplexed, lonely, weary and in many cases damaged by their experience of leadership in the local church. All this has led me to the admittedly obvious conclusion that the nurturing of leaders is a vitally important task as we contemplate the future health of the Church. 'The local church is the hope of the world, and its future rests primarily in the hands of its leaders.' (Bill Hybels)

When Paul was saying goodbye to the Leadership team in Ephesus he said this to them, by way of preparing them for their future ministry: 'Keep watch over yourselves... and all the flock of which the Holy Spirit has made you overseers.' (Acts 20.28)

So let me say something about **Leadership and Calling**. Leadership is a gift of the Holy Spirit (Romans 12.8) and a calling to serve. It is not a job, it is not a career, it is a calling. This calling, initiated by the Spirit, needs to be discerned by the whole church so that the future leader has – so to speak – no escape! In my time at St Saviour's 28 people have gone into ordained ministry. To each I said, 'If this issue will not go away, if you cannot put to rest a sense that God is on your case, then there is every chance that he is indeed calling you.' Leadership discerned must then of course be developed, and this is the work of a lifetime. Are leaders born? Well, some maybe, but most of us have to work hard to develop the necessary skills. There's a story of a group of Church leaders visiting a village in Russia. At the end of their visit one asked an old man 'Have any great leaders been born here?' The man replied, 'No, only babies.'

Then a word about **Leadership and Character.** Note carefully what Paul says, 'Keep watch over yourselves and all the flock …' We minister out of who we are. Character first, and then skills: wisdom, before technique. Did you notice what David Cameron said in his speech at the Party Conference 'Character, temperament, judgement… these come before policies and manifestos.'[2]

Michael Jinkins in his wonderful book on Church Leadership says:

> *Ministers who lead well (if we are to take Paul at his word) do not work out of their own anxiety, but out of their trust in God; they don't feed the frenzied anxiety of society (even when the frenzy of anxiety affects their congregation), but speak calmly and clearly the Word of grace and peace. They can only do this, they can only retain their sanity and balance and peace, because they have entrusted their own lives, the lives of those they love, and the lives of their enemies to the God who desires better things than we can desire.[3]*

Leaders need space and time to think, to dream, to pray, to grow. Beware of leaders who are constantly on the go 'Our Vicar gets things done' is an accolade that deeply worries me!

Finally **Leadership and the Church**. Can I offer you my VAT of leadership? **Vision**. Leaders must have vision. A major part of their calling is to stand back and see the big picture. To dream dreams, to imagine what the future might look like – and then to draw people into the realisation of those dreams and that future. This is why activism is not part of a leader's life style. Congregations must give their leaders permission to dream. Not to day-dream, not to be idle, but – Martin Luther King-like – to climb the mountain and glimpse the magnificent view on the other side. And then, **Attention**. Attention to people, their needs, their hopes, their fears. People matter more than schemes. In this sense the big-picture leader needs also to do details. Not administrative details, but detailed attention to the flock over which the Holy Spirit has made him or her overseer. The leader must connect.

Good leadership will hold in tension those two qualities of vision and attention. Where there is vision without attention, people soon feel neglected. This has happened on two occasions during my time here and it doesn't take long for the life of the Church to begin to unravel. If people feel neglected or unheard they begin to stray. 'The hungry sheep look up and are not fed' as John Milton put it. [4] Very easily the Visionary leader can become remote, and pastoral remoteness is the unpardonable sin. Spiritual vision can degenerate into personal agenda and the danger of 'leading from the front' is that sometimes the leader forgets to look round to see if anyone is following! Conversely, attention without vision is not helpful. Where the leader gets lost in pastoral details, people begin to lose a sense of direction and purpose. Care for individuals is of course never out of place, but the leader will need to learn how to delegate, and how sensitively to resist the idea that he or she is the only one who will be acceptable when a pastoral crisis breaks out. Remoteness is the unpardonable sin, but endless availability is not a wise alternative. This desire to be available at all times has its dark side. Some leaders need to be needed and some leaders are desperate to be liked. So ministry becomes an exercise in keeping everyone happy. But real pastoral compassion is about leading people beyond contentment to transformation.

To vision and attention, we must add **Truth**. The key calling is to a ministry of 'word and sacrament' and the primary focus is on the Word. Paul says to the young Timothy 'I give you this charge: Preach the Word; be prepared in season and out of season; correct, rebuke and encourage – with great patience and careful instruction.' (2 Tim 4.2) The communication of biblical truth is right at the top of the agenda. I would be bold to say that where attention is given to this, churches will grow and without it they will wither. Beneath the freneticism and frivolity of our post-modern culture there is a deep spiritual hunger. VAT: So leadership is a value added task!

If you are a leader may God bless and re-invigorate your leadership, and if you are amongst those who are being led will you pray regularly for your leader. They need your prayers more than you can ever imagine.

1. Henri J.M. Nouwen, In the name of Jesus, reflections on Christian Leadership, (DLT 2004) p.69.
2. Conservative Party Conference, Manchester 1st October 2009.
3. Transformational Ministry, Church leadership and the way of the Cross, Michael Jinkins, (St Andrew's Press 2002) p.19.
4. Lycides 1.123.

Part 3

Celebration

The Vicar's sermons at the major festivals were
tending to get a bit out of hand

Preaching is kindling the Lord's fire.'

(John Crysostom)

In many churches, Christmas morning is a full house.

Excitement levels are high with children and brand-new presents much in evidence. For many it is their once-yearly attendance, happy to be there 'for the sake of the children.' It is a great moment to tell the Christmas story and to try to get beneath the traditions to the inner meaning of the Incarnation. And to do so without manipulation, against a buzz of noise and within ten minutes. A tall order!

At our church the service lasts 45 minutes, much of it orientated directly to the children, but within it ten minutes of calm (which can be achieved if the children have already been fully engaged) to preach.

What is said needs to be direct and simple (but not simplistic.) Every word must count. I make a point of delivering this sort of sermon without notes, speaking one-to-one as it were so that everyone feels included.

The personal references about things like bread-making are so important in the process of building relationship. As well as illustrating Biblical truth they provide an insight into the preacher's normality. It's alarming to discover how often 'unchurched' people seem surprised to discover that the Vicar is human.

13. You can always come home

Some while ago Sue and I visited the town of Buxton, high in the Derbyshire Peak District. It was the town where I was born. We found the old Vicarage where life began, but the Blue plaque denoting the birth place of a famous person seemed to be missing. Perhaps it had fallen off. Nonetheless it was a sort of home-coming. I've lived in ten different houses in my 64 years and they have all been home to me.

Christmas is about coming home. 'What are you doing for Christmas?' we ask. 'Oh we're staying at home,' or 'We're spending the day with our son,' or 'The family are all coming to us.' From across the town, from across the country and sometimes from across the world families gather. Christmas is a great home-coming. Home is where the heart is, it's where we belong. At home we can be ourselves, and discover ourselves. At home we can be real! Many this Christmas will be homeless, without a home. Many will feel they could well do without the home they inhabit – because of sad memories, present tensions, future uncertainty. Sad situations, and sad because they are unnatural. This is not what is meant to be.

The Christmas story too is about a home-coming. It is about God coming to earth in the person of Jesus, to make his home here.

The word became flesh and blood,
And moved into the neighbourhood.
We saw the glory with our own eyes,
The one-of-a-kind glory,
Like father, like son:
Generous inside and out,
True from start to finish
(John 1:14 The Message)

So simple, so utterly extraordinary. That God, Creator and King, should 'move in' on planet earth and make his home here. That is the astonishing message of Christmas that we continue to hide beneath the festive trappings.

But the message is also about the invitation for us to come home to God. 'To all who received him, to those who believed in his name, he gave the right to become children of God.' Christmas is about you and me coming home to God who has come to us. And when we come to Jesus who is a **'wonderful counsellor'** we gain a new understanding of the beauty and terror of the world we inhabit. And when we come we are given strength to make a difference to the world because we come to the One who is the **'mighty God.'** Coming home to God we know again that we are loved, and we learn again how to love because he's the **'everlasting Father.'** And when we come there is peace of heart and mind – not a glassy calm but a mighty confidence because now we are made whole by the **'Prince of Peace.'** And please note: we come not because it will help us, or comfort us, or make us feel good. We come, first of all, because it is true! There is a God, and he has revealed himself, and we can know him. If you have a better explanation for the restless spiritual longing which is part of our human condition, I'd love to hear from you.

The heart of this home-coming is love: given, received and returned. Last night I was out and about delivering my customary loaves of home-made bread that every Christmas I give to church leaders and others against whom I have a grudge. Sitting at the lights at the end of Woodbridge Road, listening to Classic FM, I was suddenly aware of 'O come all ye faithful.' Aware because the choir were singing a verse we rarely sing:

> *Child for us sinners,*
> *Poor and in a manger,*
> *Fain we embrace thee*

With love and awe;
Who would not love thee,
Loving us so dearly?
O come let us adore Him ...
(Latin probably by J. F. Wade c.1743)

'Who would not love thee, loving us so dearly...' That's it. I was quite overcome and close to tears. So simple. So profound.

My father-in-law was a good, witty, wise man, and very clever. I used to sit in the front room of his bungalow in Lincolnshire and he would talk to me. He really loved me, because he would talk about economics, the state of the market, his stocks and shares, and I would listen, and never interrupt, or contradict, or question, because I hadn't a clue what he was talking about. But one day he told me about his daughter, before she became my wife. She was home from her job in the United Nations in Geneva and quite troubled and uncertain about the future. In fact unhappy (she hadn't met me yet!). Her father listened and then he said 'Look love, whatever happens you know **you can always come home.'** Five words that have become a mantra in our family (although on occasions I have been guilty of looking at my sons and thinking 'You can always **leave** home!').

You can always come home. I want to say to you this Christmas morning whatever your situation, whatever you've done, whatever your hopes or fears for 2009 – you can always come home. The door is open, the lights are on, the fire is lit, a feast is prepared and God our Father, incarnate in the Babe of Bethlehem, waits ...

The following four pieces (meditations rather than sermons) were delivered on Good Friday 2009 at the three hour service at Guildford Cathedral by kind invitation of the Dean, the Very Rev'd Victor Stock, who is a good friend.

The first two hours consisted of hymns, readings and meditations and the final hour was the Good Friday liturgy with glorious music from the choir followed by communion. The Cathedral is a splendid building – vast, light and airy. It was fairly full, which helped communication over what seemed a large expanse of marble flooring between elevated pulpit and congregation.

So – a serious time in a formal setting, with the challenge and opportunity to engage with the deepest mysteries of the faith. The meditations try to do this in a suggestive rather than an exhaustive way, inviting the congregation to do their own thinking, exploring and praying in the times of silence. The meditations contain quite a number of quotations (possibly too many) which were reproduced in an accompanying booklet.

Such services are not occasions for expansive preaching so much as quiet meditation. Again, every word counts and the talks were delivered from fairly full notes.

14.Mystery: Love, Actually

12:00-12:30 Waiting

We have three hours together. It's a very long time, it's a very short time. It is a rare opportunity to stop to reflect, to pray. William Wordsworth said: 'The world is too much with us; late and soon, getting and spending, we lay waste our powers.' [1] So here is a moment to stop, to be still, and above all, to wait.

So often we invest waiting with negative overtones. 'What are you waiting for?' we say. Or 'Don't keep me waiting' or 'I've been waiting for ages!' Sometimes I go into town with Sue, my wife. She is very quick-thinking. She will say 'I'm going into Boots for some toothpaste, you go to Smiths for the papers and I'll meet you in Marks & Spencer's, by the sandwiches, in ten minutes'. And before I can protest or check the itinerary, she's gone. So I do my job and get to Marks on time. And I wait, and I wait, and I wait .... as expectation turns into exasperation. What a waste of time. But now I've learnt better and I am never without a book of poetry in my pocket, and I'm happy to wait as long as it takes. Time need never be wasted!

We need to raise the 'stature of waiting'. [2] It ought to be a creative activity. As we wait things happen, both within us and in the world around us. We discover how refreshing it is to focus on the present moment – the only one we have. Spiritual writers of the past called it 'the sacrament of the present moment'. R. S. Thomas puts it like this:

> *Life is not hurrying*
> *on to a receding future, nor hankering after*
> *an imagined past. It is the turning*
> *aside like Moses to the miracle*
> *of the lit bush, to a brightness*
> *that seemed as transitory as your youth*
> *once, but is the eternity that awaits you.[3]*

Hurrying to a receding future, hankering after an imagined past. We all do it, and the strain it imposes shows on our worried faces. So we wait with what one writer calls 'a redemptive impotence'.

Waiting before the cross there is absolutely nothing we can do. In amazement we witness the outpouring of divine love, an act of unmerited grace. And as we allow the strain, the weariness, the anxiety and the guilt to drain away - into our receptive minds and open hands flow illumination, strength and fresh hope. 'They who wait upon the Lord shall be renewed, they shall rise up with wings like eagles, they shall run and not be weary, they shall walk and not faint' (Isaiah 40.31).

'Morgan's Passing', a novel by the American writer Anne Tyler,[4] tells the story of a disheartened old man, Morgan Gower, living in his ramshackle house in Baltimore. His wife has died, and now the last of his five daughters has left home. He is alone. Tyler describes him: 'You could say he'd gone to pieces. Perhaps he's always been in pieces. Perhaps he arrived unassembled.' Perhaps you have come to the Cathedral today, secretly and radically unassembled. The Cross is the place of reassembly – if only we will stay and wait.

Let us pray:

> *Almighty God,*
> *As we stand at the foot of the cross of your Son*
> *Help us to see and know your love for us,*
> *So that in humility, love and joy*
> *We may place at his feet*
> *All that we have and all that we are;*
> *Through Jesus Christ our Saviour.*

1. William Wordsworth, 'The World is too much within us,' (1807).
2. William Vanstone, 'The Stature of Waiting,' (DLT, 1982).
3. R.S. Thomas, 'The Bright Field' R.S. Thomas Collected Poems 1945-1990, (Phoenix Giants, 1993) p.302.
4. Anne Tyler, 'Morgan's Passing,' (Vintage, 1991) p.21.

114

15. Majesty: Scene from a Distance

12:30 – 1:00 Watching

'But all his acquaintances, including the women who had followed him from Galilee, stood at a distance, watching these things.' (Luke 23:49) Waiting, we watch, and watching, we see. In the next three reflections we will consider three partial truths about the cross, things which are often said which need further reflection.

First: 'Jesus was a helpless victim, showing on the cross God's unconditional love.'

When Jesus came to Golgotha they hanged him on a tree,
They drove great nails through hands and feet, and made a Calvary;
They crowned him with a crown of thorns, red were his wounds and deep,
For those were crude and cruel days, and human flesh was cheap.

When Jesus came to Birmingham they simply passed him by;
They never hurt a hair of him, they only let him die.
For men had grown more tender, and they would not give him pain;
They only just passed down the street and left him in the rain.

Still Jesus cried, 'Forgive them, for they know not what they do,'
And still it rained the wintry rain, that drenched him through and through.
The crowds went home and left the streets without a soul to see,
And Jesus crouched against a wall and cried for Calvary.[1]

But as we watch we see something more. Something is happening, something is being done at the cross. It is not a place of passive reaction, but of active achievement. Here, in a moment of time, death is defeated and the Kingdom of Heaven opened to all believers. Calvary is the hinge of history, an objective action so momentous that a whole world is reconciled. Not that all the world will respond, rather that grace sufficient to save and redeem a whole world is there expressed.

P. T. Forsyth, that great theologian of the cross, writes:

> *God was in Christ reconciling the world to himself, actually reconciling, finishing the work. It was not a tentative preliminary affair. Reconciliation was finished in Christ's death. Paul did not preach a gradual reconciliation. He preached what the old divines used to call the finished work. He preached something done once for all – a reconciliation which is the base of every soul's reconcilement, not an invitation only.[2]*

So, we watch this momentous event in two ways:

First, **from a distance**. Matthew, Mark and Luke make it clear in their accounts of the crucifixion that the friends of Jesus stood 'afar off'. Why so? We are not told. Maybe through fear of being seen and being implicated with Jesus of Nazareth. Maybe they just could not bear to watch the horrific scene. There is an old Saxon poem 'The Dream of the Rood' in which the poet dreams of a conversation with the tree from which the Cross is made. The tree tells its story and the climax of course is the day when it is cut down, shaped and fashioned and then raised from the earth, bearing upon itself the weight of the Son of God. 'So now I tower high and mighty under the skies, having power to heal all who will bow before me.' Calvary is an awesome place, we stand at a distance and bow the knee before the mighty love of God in Christ. Standing back, we gain perspective on the work of redemption. Watching, we feel something of the terror that gripped the soldiers when the earth shook and the rocks split and the graves burst open. 'Surely this man was the Son of God' (Matt 27:51-54). We domesticate the cross at our peril.

But then, only then, tremblingly **we draw near**. St John, as always, has a different perspective. 'Standing near the cross of Jesus were his mother, and his mother's sister, Mary the wife of Clopas, and Mary Magdalene'. So too the writer to the Hebrews sees the cross as a way opened up into the heart of the Father, giving confidence to believers to 'approach with a true heart in full assurance of faith with our hearts sprinkled clean from an evil conscience and our bodies washed with pure water.' (Heb 10:19-21) We can do so, because at the cross God in Christ has drawn near to us. He has borne our guilt and identified himself with our condition. In one of his wonderful sermons, the German theologian/preacher Helmut Thielicke imagines the Day of Judgement.

> *My name is called and I stand before the judge who asks me to give account, but before I can speak the prosecutor, Satan, interrupts: 'God, the man who stands before you, I can answer for him. He is the one who has done this and that, he has had no sympathetic love, he has overlooked his colleagues, he has served himself, he has identified with his own ambitions – he has never noticed that people right and left of him cried for help for a kind word and for a bit of mercy. He has been self-consumed'. And all this is true. But then my attorney, that is Jesus Christ, steps forward before the judge, and before I can say anything he says 'Mr Prosecutor, everything you have said is correct no longer is what he has in his background. That is really behind him. I have crossed it out, identified with him and taken it upon myself as my burden.' And he turns to the throne of judgement. 'Father and Judge, if you ask me who this is, I answer that he is the one for whom I died, and that I have suffered with him and*

because of him. I have become his brother and he has let me adopt him. He knew that his hands were empty. He knew that his conscience was stained. He knew that there was no escape from his wretchedness and he was pleased when I said to him, be clean. He accepted my offer to bear everything for him, and with him. He stood beneath my cross and said "I want to stay here by you, despise me not I pray". Therefore, Father, he is yours and mine and I bring him to you. Now he has looked to me with eyes full of grace. Look upon him now as my brother and let him be with you always in your peace and your glory." [3]

Later in the service there will be an invitation to all of us to come forward and kneel before the cross, to offer ourselves afresh to the crucified God, now risen but still bearing the marks of his passion by which we are ransomed, healed, restored and forgiven.

If we have never sought, we seek thee now;
Thine eyes burn through the dark, our only stars;
We must have sight of thorn-pricks on thy brow,
We must have Thee, O Jesus of the scars.
The other gods were strong, but Thou wast weak;
They rode, but Thou didst stumble to a throne;
But to our wounds, only God's wounds can speak,
And not a god has wounds, but Thou alone.[4]

Let us pray:

Almighty God,
Whose most dear Son went not up to joy but first he suffered pain,
And entered not into his glory before he was crucified:
Mercifully grant that we, walking in the way of the cross,
May find it none other than the way of life and peace;
Through Jesus Christ our Lord.

1. G.A. Studdert Kennedy, 'Indifference', (1883-1929).
2. P. T. Forsyth 'The Work of Christ', (Fontana, 1965) p.90.
3. Helmut Thielicke, 'I Believe – The Christian's Creed', (James Clarke & Co. Ltd).
4. Edward Shillito, 'Jesus of the Scars, and other Poems'.

16. Meekness: The Silence of the Lamb

1:00 – 1:30 Listening

Waiting, we watch and watching we listen – to the sound of silence. The second partial truth about the cross goes as follows: 'Our sin is a flaw that can easily be forgiven and forgotten.'

Coventry Patmore's moving little poem tells of the distress of a single father who in a moment of frustration with his little son sends him to bed 'with harsh words and unkissed.' Later he repents and creeps up to the bedroom and finds the boy fast asleep with tear-stains still on his cheek. On the table by his bedside he has gathered all his favourite toys for comfort.

> So when that night I prayed
> To God, I wept, and said:
> Ah, when at last we lie with trancéd breath,
> Not vexing thee in death,
> And thou rememberest of what toys
> We made our joys,
> How weakly understood
> Thy great commanded good.
> Then, fatherly, not less
> That I whom thou hast moulded from the clay,
> Thou'lt leave thy wrath, and say,
> I will be sorry for their childishness.[1]

Well, yes and no. The forgiveness of God is wonderful, free and unmerited. 'He died that we might be forgiven/He died to make us good.'

But at what cost and to whom? Sin is a serious offence against a holy God and has to be paid for so that its power can be broken. P.T. Forsyth again: 'We are not stray sheep or wandering prodigals even, we are rebels taken with weapons in our hands.'

I remember as a small boy being involved in an escapade with some of my pals which ended in a stone being thrown through a cucumber frame. The frame belonged to one of our gang's great enemies, Mr Yates. Even now, sixty years on, I can feel the excitement and terror of running up the road, I can hear Mr Yates shouting 'I've seen you, I know who you are!' Sure enough, back home my Father was waiting for me and he said, 'There, there son, I've told Mr Yates that boys will be boys and asked him to forgive and forget!' No, he didn't! He said 'Son, Mr Yates has been on the phone and I've told him you will pay for the damage, and pay in full. Now go to your room and we will talk later.' It's an inadequate illustration, but it's a start. Sin is not an unfortunate lapse to be glossed over, but a moral offence which has its effect beyond the perpetrator and needs to be addressed. So we look at the cross, and we listen. And we hear the sound of a great silence.

First, the silence of God the Father into which the Son cries out, 'My God, my God, why have you forsaken me?' This silence is bound up with the mystery of God's holiness. God's love is a holy love. His wrath is the outworking of his holy love upon sin. He is angry not in spite of his love, but because of it. God's anger against sin is not because his love is limited, but because it is unlimited. It is the holiness of God that necessitates the cross. But the mystery before which we bow deepens, because St Paul tells us that it is God himself who fulfils the conditions his holy love demands: 'God was in Christ reconciling the world to himself.' (2 Cor 5.19)

And then the silence of the Son 'God made him to be sin for us .... Behold the Lamb of God who takes away the sin of the world ... He himself bore our sins in his body on the tree.' (2 Cor 5.12, John 1.29, 1 Peter 2.24) Paul, John and Peter unite in testifying to the work of redemption accomplished in Christ who hangs in silence beneath the weight of the world's sin.

> *In the silence he absorbs the pain and the hatred that is visited upon him. The hatred and the violence will not be passed on. And although this may appear passive, such a process is strenuous and costly. In the way that Jesus endures the crucifixion a chain of consequences is broken, and the truth of forgiveness is made real.*[2]

So too our many words need to be silenced by the cross. 'I've never done any wrong, I'm good enough, God will accept me in the end.' Let the cross absorb today the chattering of our pride. Or maybe its anxiety. 'I'll never be good enough, God could never forgive me.' Before the cross of Christ all anxious thoughts can be stilled. And then there is the anger: 'Why has this happened to me?' At the cross our anger is covered by the suffering of the innocent Christ.

The vital thing is not to pretend. There are no easy answers. Consider the story of Archibald Tait who was Dean of Carlisle and later Archbishop of Canterbury. In the space of one month, March 1856, five of his daughters died in an epidemic of scarlet fever. The harrowing scene is caught in David Scott's poem 'Dean Tait.'

> *Quite put aside were any thoughts*
> *Of the state of the Cathedral roof;*
> *Instead, a quiet agony, waiting*
> *For the stethoscope's final figure of eight,*
> *And the click of the doctor's bag.*
> *He never thought there could be this routine*
> *To death: the prayer book, the size of his palm;*
> *His wife, half in doubt because of the fever,*

Hiding the sick-room drawings away;
And at their prayers each day
In a borrowed house, they tested
The bible texts against a silent nursery.[3]

Now maybe is the moment to expose our pride, our anxiety and our distress. At the cross Christ does not forgive and forget, he remembers and redeems. The silence into which we enter may not bring understanding, let alone acceptance, but it can be a first small step along the road into the sufferings of Christ.

Let us pray:

Loving God,
As we join our cries with those who in the face of your apparent
silence are in despair, renew in us the spirit of hope, the yearning
for life. In you alone is the expectancy that even when every
door is closed yet you will surprise us with joy.
Through Christ our Lord,
Amen.

1. Coventry Patmore, (1823-1896) 'The Toys.'
2. Martyn Percy, 'The Silence of the Lamb' quoted in Darkness Yielding, Liturgies, Prayers and Reflections (Canterbury Press, 2007) p.149.
3. David Scott, 'Selected Poems,' (Bloodaxe Books, 1998) p.47 quoted in 'Seven Words for the 21st Century' (DLT, 2002) p.59.

17. Momentum:

Such a fast God

1:30 – 2:00 Travelling
Waiting, watching, listening – then, and then only, are we ready to move.

The third partial truth we need to examine is the idea that the cross is simply an object of contemplation, a sort of retreat or even a final resting place. A Victorian hymn, Beneath the Cross of Jesus, catches the mood. Here is the final verse:

> *O Christ, beneath thy shadow*
> *Be my abiding-place:*
> *I ask no other sunshine than*
> *The sunshine of thy face;*
> *Content to let the world go by,*
> *And count its gain but loss;*
> *This sinful self my only shame,*
> *My only hope thy cross.*
> (Elizabeth Clephane c.1868, 'Beneath the Cross of Jesus')

But as we stand beneath the cross, waiting, watching, listening, there will arise within us a passion not to let the world go by. Rather a divine discontent will build within us, a momentum to go to the broken world. A better hymn is: 'Lift high the cross, the love of Christ proclaim/ Til all the world adores his sacred name.' (George W. Kitchin)

Here are some stirring words by the German theologian, Jurgen Moltmann:

> *The symbol of the cross in the church points to the God who was*
> *crucified not between two candles on an altar, but between two*

thieves at the place of the skull, where outcasts belong, outside the gates of the city .... It is a symbol which therefore leads out of the Church, and out of religious longing into the fellowship of the oppressed and the abandoned. [1]

So what are we to do? Can I suggest 3 simple steps?

Be aware of the state of our culture, of which of course we as believers are a part, but to which we are called to go with the message of the cross. Our culture is not so much secular as pagan, not just homeless, but homesick. Deep within society's amnesia about the Christian Gospel and a mindset that tells us consumerism is the essence of human identity, there persistently lurks a strain of spiritual longing. We should not be surprised for 'Thou hast made us for thyself and our hearts are restless till they rest in thee.' (St. Augustine) To respond well, we must first understand. Waiting this afternoon beneath the cross let us ask for a new awareness of the pain of our world, and a fresh understanding of the contours of that pain.

Believe in the power of the cross to reassemble people. And that belief must be discovered and incarnated in the Church. Listen to these hard words:

> *How has it happened that people who speak with such conviction and assurance about the atonement often show such little evidence in daily life, or in interpersonal relationships, of a crucified mind? Why are orthodox Christian Churches and organisations, with belief in the atonement of Christ enshrined in doctrinal statements that are binding on their members, so often riven by ugly divisions resulting from human pride, anger and intolerance? And why is the message of the cross so often reduced to a private affair, a treasure confined to religious rituals, with no obvious connection to the agonies and spiritual hunger of a watching world?* [2]

Not until we feel and experience the power of the cross in our corporate life will we be able with any integrity to lift it high in the world. 'You Christians must look more redeemed, if I am to believe in your redeemer' said the atheist philosopher, Nietzsche. It calls for the church to display a crucified mind, and not a crusading one. We will need to put to death much of our cherished power and authority.

Make connection: Let's end with the image of darkness and light, and the idea that the proclamation of the cross will bring light, illumination and hope. When Robert Louis Stevenson was a little boy he was standing one day at the window of his nursery on the first floor of his Edinburgh home. He was watching the lamplighter moving down the street with his ladder and his taper lighting, one by one, the gas lamps. 'What are you doing?' said his nurse. 'Watching that man knocking holes in the darkness' replied the little boy.

It's as simple as that and as challenging. The momentum the church needs is energy to lift high the cross so that its light will pierce the darkness of our world.

> *Saviour of Calvary,*
> *Costliest victory,*
> *Darkness defeated*
> *And Eden restored;*
> *Born as a man to die,*
> *Nailed to a cross on high,*
> *Cold in the grave to lie,*
> *Jesus is Lord!*
>
> *Source of all sovereignty,*
> *Light, immortality,*
> *Life everlasting*
> *And heaven assured;*
> *So with the ransomed, we*

Praise him eternally,
Christ in his majesty,
Jesus is Lord!
(Timothy Dudley-Smith b.1926)

Let us pray:
Almighty God,
Who called your Church to witness
that you were in Christ
reconciling the world to yourself:
Help us so to proclaim the good news of your love,
that all who hear it
may be reconciled to you;
through him who died for us and rose again
and reigns with you and the Holy spirit,
one God, now and forever
Amen.

Amen.

1. Jurgen Moltmann, 'The Crucified God,' (Fortress Press, 1993) p.40.
2. David Smith, 'Against the Stream,' (IVP, 2003) p.123.

View from the Pew

Preaching is a gift of God. It is about opening windows in our minds and spirits, to reveal a kingdom that is not of this world, to lift our eyes up to discover a God of grace and kindness, to discover the God 'who creates the world in love, redeems the world in suffering and will consummate the world in joyous well-being' (Brueggemann). We learn to hope in an awesome God. Our minds are enlarged and our world-view is challenged.

At the same time, a good preacher is a pastoral theologian, always asking, 'What difference does this truth from Scripture make to the lives of my people here, at this time and in this place?' In this our preacher stands with us, alongside us, in our frailty, experiencing the same emotions, living the same life of trusting faith in God. With humour, with stories and parables, and with humility she or he shares our life, and brings Scripture alive in its relevance to each one of us.

Good preaching comes from a profound sense of God's word for us today: God's word is living and active, to comfort and heal, as well as to direct and form us into a people passionate and single-heartedly devoted to a holy God and his purposes. We are formed to become 'the local church - the hope of the world'.

A revolving door in the entrance to a grand building serves as an image. We enter through the door into our community, to read Scripture, listen to sermons, study, pray, be filled with the Spirit. And then we must go out, back through the revolving door, to take God's love to his broken world, to serve, in whichever way we have been called, and to love the world for His sake and in Christ's name.

Marion De Quidt

When I was a child, Easter was observed as the major festival of the Christian Year.

In our local church, no one dreamt of going away for Easter: It was a time to celebrate at home and, in all probability, to parade a new set of clothes. The proceeds of the collection plate were given as a gift to the Vicar: 'The Easter Offertory'. Those were the days! All has changed. Easter remains theologically the central festival, but in popularity of observance it has been well outstripped by Christmas.

In our church many people are away on holiday or visiting family, but by the same token many visitors join us. So, one way or another, attendance holds up.

Like Christmas, it is a moment to tell the 'story of our redemption', bearing in mind that many will be in church who are not committed in heart or mind to that story. So the facts need to be told simply, which means that the preacher needs to reflect deeply. It is another moment for direct communication without recourse to notes if possible.

The Resurrection narratives are vivid and alive – as are the post-Resurrection appearances. To bore people at Easter would be a major achievement.

The present sermon, based on the story of Jesus' appearance on the seashore recorded in John 21, was a particular challenge to Christians to renew their allegiance to the risen Christ.

18.King of the World

This time last year, the family went to Cornwall for a holiday by the sea. We went on Easter Monday, and early-ish on Tuesday morning I went down to the sea shore. I was feeling relaxed. Holy Week (six sermons preached in Aberystwyth!) and Easter Day at St Saviour's were over. 'Your busy time of year, Vicar' people unhelpfully say with the unspoken assumption that for the rest of the year you are a clerical layabout!

There's something very special, very haunting, about the morning light on the sea and I was so glad to be there. It is interesting that one of the Resurrection appearances is on a cold, bleak spring morning by the Sea of Galilee. Seven of the disciples were there and the mood was one of doubt, confusion, even despondency. They had seen Jesus alive but then he had disappeared and they were still not sure what they were supposed to do. It was like 'now you see me, now you don't' and they were confused and despondent. Peter says, 'I'm going fishing'. Peter, who always abhorred a vacuum. Ready to go back to something he knew and understood. Back to the old job. Back to doing something, rather than just waiting around. And the rest of them, as usual, followed his lead. 'We will come with you.'

I wonder how you feel this morning? I wonder if there is any despondency here? Perhaps things haven't turned out the way you expected or hoped for and you are not sure what to do next. So we do what we know best. 'Let's go to Tesco, let's think about changing the car, let's book a holiday, let's tidy the garden (you must be desperate!). Then I'll feel better'. No you won't! That night the disciples went out and caught nothing.

And as dawn breaks Jesus is standing on the shore. He is always there – on the shore-line of our lives. So he comes and he calls across the water 'Try fishing on the other side.' Reluctantly they obey, and when the net is raised it is so full it nearly breaks. I wonder if the disciples remembered a similar occasion (recounted in Luke chapter 5)? Jesus perhaps evokes their memories to prove it really is him, he is alive. On the shore they are embarrassed because they know him but they don't know him and they put their heads down. But then breakfast is prepared and they sit round the fire and eat the fish that Jesus has prepared. He prays over the fish, using the same words he used when they fed the five thousand, and suddenly the disciples recognise his presence: gathered around their master, they are clarified and reassembled. They would never doubt again, they had seen him and now they were with him. They were eating breakfast together, he had come back into the ordinariness of their lives and marked them with his risen presence. So the church of Jesus Christ in every age needs to reassemble itself around the risen Christ, and the fire of his love. Then, and only then, will we be ready to tell the good news of his risen life.

Now the story moves on. The moment Peter has longed for and has been dreading has arrived. Three times Peter had denied Jesus and now, the breakfast things cleared away, Jesus says 'Peter, do you love me, do you love me, do you love me?' Peter replies, 'You know I am your friend.' That was all he could manage but it is enough. Jesus tells him that he is loved, reinstated and commissioned. 'Feed my sheep.' Here is a carpenter telling a fisherman to become a shepherd. It is all so personal, and this morning you are face to face with Christ, who loves you too much to let you escape. 'William, Mary, John, Sarah, Sam. I want to recommission you, I want to set you on your feet, I want to dispel your despondency, I want to clarify your mind. We have so much to do together'. Face to face encounter. The Christian faith is never individualist, but it is always personal.

On Thursday evening, Sue and I went to Heathrow to collect our son, Robert, back from three months in South Africa, not bad work if you can get it. As each face emerged out of the baggage hall, we looked and it was not the right face, and then suddenly it **was** the right face, cheerful, chubby, cheeky Robert, and we embraced him. 'Welcome home, Robert, despite everything, welcome home.' And Jesus, face to face with you this morning, says 'Welcome home.' For every denial there is an assurance of love and grace. Christ wants to make us shepherds so we can go and feed his sheep.

So the message is for the whole church and the message is for you. The message is that we need to lay down our fears, our despondency, our disappointment, our sadness, our anger, our broken dreams and our unrealised ambitions, and open ourselves afresh to Christ who is King of the world that we may follow him joyfully this Easter time. We lay ourselves down that he may take us up.

A final story, listen carefully. In 1924 Evelyn Underhill was addressing a number of eminent politicians and economists at the University of Manchester. She ended her speech with this story.

There was once a Brownie who lived in a wood. He had a little wheelbarrow and passed his time in a very moral and useful manner picking up slugs and snails. Yet there was something lacking in his life. The King of the World passed through that wood very early every morning and made all things beautiful and new but the Brownie had never seen him. He longed to, but something prevented it. He had one cherished possession, a lovely little green blanket which had fallen one day out of the fairy queen's chariot and which he had not been able to help keeping for himself. It was very cold in the wood at night but the blanket kept him so warm and cosy that he never woke up to see the King of the World. And one day there came to him a Shepherd who looked deep into the soul of the Brownie and said to him, 'Haven't you seen the King of the World?' And the Brownie said, 'No, I do so want to, but somehow I can't manage it.' Then the Shepherd replied, 'But I seem to see something in your soul that keeps you from the vision; something that looks rather like a blanket.' And at that a terrible fight began in the heart of the Brownie between wanting to go on being warm and comfortable in his blanket and longing to see the King of the World.

'Perhaps,' added Evelyn Underhill, 'the ultimate choice which lies before us may turn out to be the Brownie's choice between the Heavenly Vision and the blanket.'[1]

That was the choice Evelyn Underhill placed before her distinguished audience. And it is the choice I offer this morning to this distinguished congregation. What is the green blanket which means so much to you that you are prepared to trade it for a vision of the risen Christ? May I invite you this Easter morning to lay down your green blanket of ambition, of fear, of bitterness, of sadness, of guilt, that you may see the King of the World and hear his words of forgiveness and commission. Then we shall go out joyfully to proclaim until that day when we see face to face.

1. Evelyn Underhill, 'Looking into the Soul,' quoted in 'The Quiet Heart, Prayers and Meditations for each day of the year,' ed. George Appleton, (Fount 1983) p.83.

Another set of notes lost — another
off-the-cuff sermon

If Christmas has superseded Easter in the Christian festival popularity chart, Pentecost is almost a non-starter, ranking below Harvest and Remembrance.

So the sermon is likely to be addressed to the faithful, an opportunity for the renewal of Christian discipleship.

For Christians it is, of course, a major festival. On the eve of his crucifixion, Jesus taught his disciples about the coming of the Spirit who would enlighten and empower the Church for the mission of God in the world. Jesus told them to wait for the gift of the Spirit who would give power to witness. He also spoke of the Spirit as Advocate and Comforter, the one who would come alongside, deepening understanding of the truth and enlarging vision for a lost world.

Power and Passion.

So these two words are never far from my mind when preaching on the Spirit, and Pentecost is a moment to take up the challenge to preach with power and passion-and not just on this day, but on all occasions.

19.New Life

I love the story of the road to Emmaus. The novelist George Eliot called it 'The most beautiful story in the world'. It's a long narrative taking up the whole of Luke 24. Our focus tonight is the final verses, often neglected (36-49).

The situation is as follows: Jesus has revealed himself to the two disciples at Emmaus. They recognise him and are so startled and energised that they run back to Jerusalem – 7 miles. There they meet the eleven disciples (Judas has now gone) and their stories mingle excitedly: *'You'll never guess, we've seen Jesus alive!'* *'So have we,'* reply the others. And as they are talking it happens again. Jesus comes. The disciples are terrified. They think He is a ghost. Jesus says, 'Look. A ghost does not have flesh and blood as you see I have'. He calls for food; trembling they provide some fish and He eats it in front of them. He says *'If only you had read the scriptures, if only you had thought, reflected, believed, you would not be surprised. The Messiah will suffer and die, and rise and then the Kingdom of God will be proclaimed throughout the World beginning in Jerusalem. And listen – you are to do the job. Wait, you thought I was a ghost – wait and I will send upon you the Holy Ghost, the Spirit, who will fill you with power to bear witness to me.'*

Some weeks later it happened. The day of Pentecost came and the disciples were transformed, spilling boldly onto the streets of the city, setting out to turn their world upside down.

And now it's 2008 and we gather as they did. 'The Lord is here, His Spirit is with us'. If you belong to Christ, you know that the Spirit already lives in you. He has brought you to faith in Christ. He has given you gifts to exercise. He is developing in you the fruit of love, joy,

137

peace, patience, kindness, which is growing slowly, maybe painfully, in your life and mine. So, we have the Spirit. But listen. The Spirit who already dwells in us longs to come to us again – to overwhelm us, to enlighten us, to strengthen us, to bring new life so that we may go and serve Christ well. The Spirit who is with us longs to keep coming to us. Like the first disciples we are invited to wait until the power is released.

When the Spirit comes He will do two things:
First, He will bring us to a **new aliveness**. How alive do you feel tonight? You look OK to me. But maybe someone would say 'David, I feel inside more dead than alive.' The Spirit's work is to bring you alive again. T.S. Eliot's lines in 'Murder in the Cathedral' express the apathy with which perhaps many can identify:

> *We do not wish anything to happen.*
> *Seven years we have lived quietly,*
> *Succeeded in avoiding notice,*
> *Living and partly living.*
> *There have been oppression and luxury,*
> *There have been poverty and licence,*
> *There has been minor injustice.*
> *Yet we have gone on living,*
> *Living and partly living.*

How different when we come alive, alert, responsive! Bishop J. V. Taylor in his magnificent little book 'A Matter of Life and Death' puts it like this:

> *If you pick up an old brown tennis ball from the long grass and in the palm of your hand it wriggles, you drop it quick. When you see it is only the children's hamster on the loose again your alarm seems ridiculous. But at the moment of contact when you realised 'It's alive!' your reaction was prompt – so was the hamster's.*

Taylor goes on... 'What evidence is there that we Christians are partakers of life and will share his resurrection unless it be some more intense aliveness in us here and now?'[1]

I pray that the Holy Spirit will descend again upon the people in whom He dwells, causing us to bubble with new life, bringing us alive to the reality of the living God who rules over all and whose purposes are good and true. Alive to the pain and beauty of our broken world and the specific challenges of our own community, alive to the wonderful challenges of discipleship as we see again that, beyond our belief in God, He believes in us and has called us 'for such a time as this'. An aliveness that challenges my natural self-preservation, my sad caution and cynicism, causing me to move out of my comfort zone, to take risks, to meet people, to cross bridges, to break down barriers, to oppose all that sets itself up in opposition to the reign of God. So the Holy Spirit came on the Emmaus Road causing the hearts of the disciples to burn within them.

That heavenly Teacher sent from God
Shall your whole soul inspire,
Your mind shall fill with sacred truth,
Your heart with sacred fire.

Secondly, when the Holy Spirit comes He will bring **new awareness.** Our aliveness in Christ brings an awareness of His world and the call upon our lives to live to his praise and glory. 'You are witnesses of these things. And see, I am sending upon you what my Father promises .....' And when the Spirit came they went out. Out of the safe retreat of the upper room onto the hostile streets of Jerusalem. Out of this lovely church into the town of Guildford. 'Wait in the City' says the Risen Christ and then at Pentecost they go. Luke records in Acts 8 that Philip goes to the city of Samaria and proclaims Christ. Many believed - and then this: 'So there was great joy in that City'. (8.8)

So on this Pentecost evening the challenge to us all is very simple. Are we prepared to open ourselves to the coming of the Spirit and to the disturbing aliveness He brings and to the awareness of a city in need of joy, in need of Christ? Do we have a vision for Guildford, to bring joy and hope to our fragile, fearful culture?

Life is stronger than death. Many things in our society tend to death: the death of hope, of expectation, of desire, of marriages, of relationships. Christ who has conquered death brings life. And life is stronger than death. Many of us were in Stoke Park at lunchtime having a church picnic. Someone said: 'Just look over there at that tree against the sky'. It was magnificent – a lime tree – glorious gentle green against a fierce blue sky. It filled the horizon and all the leaves had unfurled. The power of life. Year upon year winter gives place to spring, death to new life. So the life of the Spirit comes to banish our deadness, bringing life and awareness and power so that we can bear witness to the Lord of life and death.

Can you catch this vision? 'I think so David, but please tell me what I should do to come alive again?' Here's a picture as we conclude. It's a big lake and on the shoreline are three boats, a motor boat, a rowing boat and a sail boat. How do you get to the other side? Many Christians leap into the motor boat. 'Christ is in us, the hope of glory. I can sit back and all will be well. He will carry me safely to the other side. I'm on my way to heaven and I will not be moved.' Is that you? If so, you're in the wrong boat. Beware! Paul says, 'Work out your own salvation in fear and trembling.' (Phil.2.12)

Some Christians gravitate to the rowing boat. They are the activists, the ones who believe that everything depends on them. They grit their teeth as they row in all weathers, striving to get to the other side. Is that you? Please listen. You do not have to build the Kingdom. It already exists – our task is to bear witness, to unveil the presence of Christ. Paul says, in the very next verse '... it is God that works in you to do his good pleasure.'

Listen – it's the sail boat. You get in and there is plenty to do, all that pulling of ropes and tackle as you move out onto the lake. The wind is blowing, you hoist your sail and the wind catches it and you move through the water. That's it. That is the authentic life of discipleship. This is life in the Spirit. Let God fill your sails. It is the most exhilarating experience. You are ready, you are available, you have made preparation and now the wind is blowing and the Spirit will take you into all the places He has prepared that you may bear witness to Jesus Christ, crucified, risen, reigning and gloriously alive.

Blow, thou cleansing wind from heaven,
Burn, thou fire, within our hearts.
Spirit of the Lord, possess us,
Fill our lives in every part.
Mind of Christ, be thou our ruler,
Word of truth, be thou our guide;
Leave no part of us unhallowed.
Come, O come, in us abide.

Fill thy church, inspire and strengthen,
Chasten, mould, empower and lead.
Make us one, and make us joyful,
Give us grace for every need.
Be our life, build firm thy kingdom.
Be our strength, who are but frail.
Then indeed against us never
Shall the gates of hell prevail.

Win the world! Baptize the nations!
Open every blinded eye.
Leave no sinner unconvicted;
Leave no soul untouched and dry.
Conquering love, take thou the kingdom,
Rule thou over all our days;
Then in glory and rejoicing
Earth shall echo with thy praise.

1. J.V. Taylor, 'A Matter of Life and Death,' (SCM Press, 1986) p.17

Part 4

Renewal

The church visitor felt particularly alienated this morning

'Sunday morning is for some, a last, desperate hope that life need not be lived in alienation.'

(Walter Brueggemann)

We all have our favourite parts of Scripture – and mine is St John's Gospel.

The following five sermons formed a connected series preached in the Spring of 2009: four at St Saviour's and one (no.21) at Guildford Cathedral.

The sermons highlight some of the vivid human settings of John's story of Jesus: a miracle, an encounter, a saying, a prayer and a promise. Beneath the surface of the narrative there are hidden depths – and the deeper we go into John the more challenging are the lessons of discipleship to be learned.

It is a good analogy to preaching. The sermon must engage at a human level, but then draw the hearer deeper into the truth revealed and its practical implications for discipleship.

The first sermon is the wedding at Cana, with the challenge to allow the Spirit of God so to invade our lives that they will sparkle like wine, bringing joyful satisfaction to the world around!

20.Finest Wine

Everyone loves a wedding. They are great occasions.They fill your heart with joy and gladness, unless it's one of your children being married, in which case they empty your pockets of money. The first public act of Jesus recorded by John is the wedding at Cana. 'There was a wedding at Cana of Galilee and Jesus and his disciples were invited to the wedding.' (2:1.) It's an eastern wedding, probably going on for days, maybe even weeks. The whole village would be invited and very likely most of the rival village of Nazareth. Central to the festivities, then as now, was the provision of wine. And at Cana, disaster of disasters, it ran out.

You can imagine the panic. Mary turns instinctively to her son and says 'What are we going to do?' Jesus gives this rather strange reply, to which we will return: 'What is that to you and me? My time has not yet come.' Mary goes to the servants: *I don't know what is going on. It's a disaster. But whatever he says to you – do it.'* Then Jesus turns to the servants and says 'See these water jars. Fill them to the brim with water.' And once they are filled, the water becomes wine. That is the miracle. The wine overflows, disaster is averted, all is well. End of story. So simple, except that it is John telling the story, and with John nothing is ever simple. There are layers of meaning.

So what is going on? It is a story about transformation, on lots of levels. The transformation of water into wine, of disaster into success, of fear into faith as the miracle unfolds. 'Jesus did this, the first of his signs, and revealed his glory; and his disciples believed in him.' (2:11) There are seven miracles recorded in the Gospel. John calls them signs because he wants us to understand that, behind the act of compassion that motivates them, there is a message being given, for those with eyes to see, that here the Kingdom of God is breaking in. In the actions of this enigmatic prophet called Jesus of Nazareth God's powerful presence is being unveiled. Here heaven is touching earth. Right at the end of chapter 1 there is the meeting between Jesus and Nathaniel where Jesus reveals his knowledge of Nathaniel. Nathaniel is astonished and blurts out 'How can this be? You must be the Son of God, the King of Israel.' (1:40) Jesus tells him that he's seen nothing yet and then refers to the Old Testament story (Gen. 28) of God's appearing to Jacob. In his dream Jacob sees a ladder let down from heaven with angels climbing on it, representing the presence of God. Jesus is saying that his presence is bringing the life of heaven to earth: 'You will see heaven opened and the angels of God ascending and descending upon the Son of Man.' (1:51)

Let's begin with the water jars. There are six of them, holding about 25 gallons each – so this is some wedding! Please note that the jars are empty. They are sacred jars put there, says John, for the purification rites of the Jews, and they are empty. John wants us to understand that the old Jewish system is empty. It can no longer deliver spiritual truth and power. It is a system waiting for the arrival of the Messiah, Jesus the Son of God, the Saviour of the world. So the jars are empty, but then at the command of Jesus they are filled with water that becomes wine. Jesus has come to transform and renew a tired religious system. Not to abolish it, but to fulfil it. He does not say 'The jars are empty, let us smash them and I will pour new wine miraculously from heaven.' He says 'Here are the old jars that are empty and have reached the end of their usefulness; let us fill them with water, the sign of human life, and I will transform that water into wine.'

Here is a powerful message if we are prepared to receive it. There is barrenness in the institutional Church, there is a lack of life, of vitality, of power, and the poor old Church of England needs to be filled again with the Spirit of God. It is a personal message as well. Maybe you have come this morning and you have a belief in God, you are regular in your attendance at church, you say your prayers, you do your best – but, truth to tell, you feel like an empty jar. You have not told anyone but that is how you are feeling, and you have gone as far as you can in your attempt to get right with God, but somehow nothing seems to change. Certainly you do not feel that you are sparkling like wine! And Jesus comes to his church, to you and me, and he says 'I want to break into your structures, into all that you regularly and devoutly do, and I want to breathe life into you. I want to come to you personally. I don't want to shatter you, to change the personality I have created. But I want to fill all that you uniquely are – created in my image – that you may become all that I can see that you can be. I want you to sparkle like wine.'

> *Wisdom unsearchable, God the invisible,*
> *Love indestructible in frailty appears;*
> *Lord of infinity, stooping so tenderly,*
> *Lifts our humanity to the heights of his throne.*[1]

Isn't that good? God loves all he has made, and he wants to pour himself into you and transform you. 'I want to come to David Bracewell with his warm smile, and his northern accent, and his long sermons and I want to fill him that he may become, by my grace, all that I intend him to be.'

Two questions present themselves. Here is the first: What will a church, a disciple, look like when filled with the life of God? Well, three things, at least, will be evident. First there will be **integrity.** Facing a broken world we need to sparkle with integrity. Our words needs to be true, our actions consistent, our promises fulfilled. We need to be people who can be trusted – and never more than at this moment in our country. There is a deep need for trustworthiness in private and public life.[2]

Secondly, there will be **imagination**; the exercise of imagination in our understanding of the Gospel, its simplicity and its complexity. We too often think we have the Gospel parcelled up and we proclaim it like a cheap bargain-basement offer – too good to refuse. But it is not like that. The good news of redemption is intensely simple and wonderfully complex. And then imagination in understanding our culture, which at one level seems unaware and uninterested in God, yet at another displays a persistent longing for spiritual reality. Our post-modern culture is not so much secular as pagan. If someone turns to you tomorrow for wisdom, if someone wanders into St Saviour's, what will be offered? Tepid water will not do. They need vintage wine.

Then thirdly, a church filled with the Spirit is a church of **intensity,** by which I mean passion. We are to be a passionate people. I know it is the Home Counties, but we need passion. The rather gloomy Danish theologian, Soren Kierkegaard, once said, 'Jesus did a miracle in Cana of Galilee, by turning water into wine. The Church has performed a far greater miracle. It has taken the wine of the Gospel and turned it into water.' May God have mercy on our institutional souls. May he bring us alive by the Spirit. May we sparkle like wine. There is a novel by Jeanette Winterson called 'The Passion' set in an imaginary 19th century France. One of the characters, a young man, has been pursuing a headstrong woman without success. 'When I told her mother what had happened, she stopped her baking. "You're too steady for her, she goes for madmen. I tell her to calm down but she never will. She wants it to be Pentecost everyday." ' Passion. Do you want it to be Pentecost every day?

There is a second question. 'How are we to be filled with the Spirit? How does water become wine?' Three phrases in the story are significant. Mary says to Jesus 'They have no wine.' (v.3) It's the perfect prayer. Clear, honest, direct. No beating about the bush, no convoluted religious phraseology: 'They have no wine.' If we are to be filled again there must be honesty. 'God, we are empty, we need you. We have no wine – only tepid water.' It's very simple, isn't it? Then Mary says to the servants 'Do whatever he tells you.' Again – it's not rocket science. To honesty, add obedience. If we want to be filled with the Spirit of God, with the wine of his presence, we had better do what he says. For thirty years Sue has said to me: 'Just do what I say and your life will be so much easier and more enjoyable!'

Then, this strange sentence from Jesus to his mother: 'Dear woman, what is this to you and me? My time has not yet come.' Honesty, obedience and then the humility and willingness to wait. God is sovereign and his timing is perfect. He looks for our honesty, he waits for our obedience –but then he requires our trust. 'God, we are ready. Will you bring us alive again by your Spirit? May we sparkle like wine. But, patiently, we await your moment.'

One final thought. When the master of ceremonies tastes the water that has become wine he is overwhelmed. He goes to the bridegroom: *'What is going on here? Normally we begin with Chardonnay and then we serve the plonk. But you have saved the quality wine to the end.'*

Two things. Wine matures. Listen. The further you go on the Christian way the better it can get. And the older you get the more mature you can become in Christ. Mike Thornton – isn't that true? You are nearly 90 and still going strong. We have had so many adventures together in the service of Jesus and you are still here. You look wonderful.[4] But in secular society it is very different. As you grow older you are often overlooked, and discounted. You are past your sell-by date. Experience and maturity count for little and in our fast- moving world youthfulness is everything. How different the values of the Kingdom of God! Paul puts it like this: 'Outwardly we are wasting away...' In time your teeth drop out, your hearing fades, your hair thins, your limbs stiffen. But listen, listen: 'Outwardly you are wasting away, but inwardly you are being renewed...' (2 Cor 4:16) We are on our way to 'an eternal weight of glory.' We are being filled day by day, and this is the work of the Lord who is the Spirit.

Secondly, wine is for drinking. Day by day we are maturing in Christ. And day by day we are being poured out, to satisfy the thirst of a watching world, to bring light where there is darkness, to bring joy where there is sadness, to bring hope where there is despair. Wine is for drinking. The Gospel is to be shared. And like the first disciples, those who come under our sparkling influence will see an unveiling of the glory of Jesus, and come to put their trust in him.

May it be so, for his name's sake.

1. Graham Kendrick, 'Meekness and Majesty,' (1986).
2. The sermon was preached just as the MP's expenses scandal was beginning to surface.
3. Jeanette Winterson, 'The Passion,' (Vintage, 1996) p.122.
4. Mike Thornton was my church warden when I first came to Guildford and he has remained a faithful colleague and very dear friend over 25 years of ministry.

These are a few words spoken before the sermon, not directly relating to its theme, but a spontaneous desire to tell the congregation how I was feeling.

As you know the Bracewell family are in transition, preparing to leave at the end of the year. People keep saying to me, very kindly, 'Where are you going to live? What are you going to do? Where will you worship?' The answer is a thrice-repeated 'I don't know'. We have been serving cream teas at the Rectory for the past few weeks – a sort of extended farewell. Exhausting, but great fun. I now know that one thing I will not be doing in retirement is running a teashop! Again the question about the future was asked and I said the uncertainty was a bit frightening. Back came the reply: 'Well, for twenty five years you have told us all to live by faith – come and join your congregation!'

So I want you to know that your Rector has feet of clay – you knew that anyway – and we are a bit scared of an uncertain future, but deep down we are held in the hands of a loving God and we know that 'all will be well and all manner of things shall be well.'

21.Belonging to the Kingdom

We come again to the fabulous gospel of John. The more we dig into it the more incredible it becomes. We started last week with a miracle, now we are going to look at an encounter.

Let's picture the scene. It is night-time on the Mount of Olives. Two men are standing on the lower slopes together. The wind is blowing up the valley rustling the leaves in the olive trees as they stand face to face. One man is an eminent theologian, a man of standing in the community, a man assured of his position, but not unkind. The other is a wandering Rabbi, not properly trained but remarkably effective and increasingly popular. Someone has said that when reading the Synoptic Gospels you get a very factual view of Jesus' life and ministry, and then you come to John and you get a more intimate insight about what is going on beneath the surface. It is like the difference between watching the 10 o'clock news and listening to a chat show.

The chat show of John 3 is between Nicodemus and Jesus. So Nicodemus comes and he wants to talk about the Kingdom of God. Nicodemus, urbane, measured, self-assured, slightly condescending. He has been a spectator of the signs that Jesus has done, and has been impressed by his personality. So he says, 'Rabbi, we know that you are a teacher who has come from God for no-one could perform the miraculous signs that you are doing if God were not with him ... *Jesus, we teachers, we professionals, we have been talking about you and we think you are doing very well. You could have a promising career.'* In reply Jesus says, 'Nicodemus, unless a man is born again he cannot see the Kingdom of God.' The sub-text seems to be *'Nicodemus, I have no time for carefully worded compliments, too much is at stake.'* This dialogue is gritty, direct, provocative. Nicodemus, the urbane theologian, is looking for enlightenment. Jesus, the radical Rabbi, is offering regeneration. 'You must be born again.' And he starts to talk to Nicodemus about the Kingdom of God.

I want to ask three questions by way of getting to the heart of this encounter. The first question is this: **What is meant by the Kingdom of God?** Can we remind ourselves, very briefly, of the New Testament teaching about the Kingdom? First, it is not a location; it is not a place 'above the bright blue sky.' The Kingdom is where the King is. Secondly, the Kingdom has already come. It is being inaugurated in Jesus the Messiah. It will not be consummated until the end of the age - Nicodemus was quite right. It is about the future. But what will one day finally come is already appearing, being unveiled, in the person of Jesus, the Son of God. What the theologians call the now and the not yet. The Kingdom has arrived and it is yet to come. It has come in the person of Jesus, but one day it will be finally consummated when the 'kingdoms of this world shall become the kingdoms of our Lord and of his Christ and he shall reign for ever and ever.' (Rev 11.15) Alleluia! So thirdly, the Church lives in the overlap, a foretaste of the Kingdom, reflecting, in our common life, kingdom values in a broken world. We partake of that brokenness yet we point to another way, a future hope, another world where what is now broken will be mended. We proclaim the values of the Kingdom of God in a world that has largely rejected them.

I was very interested to read a little piece by Rowan Williams, the Archbishop of Canterbury, in The Times yesterday, talking about the ongoing expenses scandal. In his typical, very delicate and penetrating way, he was suggesting that we need to beware of too much pressure lest, in our ongoing determination to nail every single politician, we really do begin to lose the thread in terms of our hope for the democratic process generally. However, he went on to say that there was a serious moral issue and he put it this way. He said that whenever a politician comes on television and says 'What I did was within the rules', then virtue is being replaced by regulation. 'Because the rules have been kept I am not morally culpable.' It was a window for me into this business of the Kingdom and the world. The people who live in the Kingdom of God say to a broken world 'Virtue goes before regulation.' There is a deeper thing than keeping your nose clean and getting away with it. It is acting with integrity, whatever it may cost. These are Kingdom values. One small example of what it is to live Kingdom values in a world that does not acknowledge the King. So Jesus begins to teach this learned theologian some of the basic rules about the Kingdom of God. *'Nicodemus, the Kingdom of God will come, but, Nicodemus, I want you to understand that the Kingdom of God is before you in my person and, Nicodemus, I do not want you to assume that you belong because you are a theologian, because you are an accepted man in the community.'*

So that leads us to our second question: **How do I qualify for inclusion in the Kingdom?** Nicodemus thinks he knows. The Kingdom will come at the end of the age and he, Nicodemus, will qualify for inclusion because of his theological standing, his race, his background, his standing in the community. Jesus challenges him. He wants Nicodemus to understand that the Kingdom has already come and is confronting him on the Mount of Olives and that his entrance into it has nothing to do with his credit rating. 'Nicodemus, you must be born again.' Listen very carefully. I belong to the Kingdom because I am in Christ. What were we singing earlier? 'In Christ alone my hope is found, he is my light, my strength, my song.' I am uniquely created by the hand of the Father, redeemed on the cross through the sacrifice of the Son, and now indwelt by the Holy Spirit. I am a man in Christ – accepted, redeemed, set free to belong and serve.

In three weeks' time I'm off to Sheffield to teach young Church leaders on something called "The Arrow Leadership Course". They have asked me to send some biographical details. They want a picture of me (oh dear!). They want to know my qualifications and a little bit about me and what I have done. It won't take long. It matters and it doesn't matter. It matters that they know a bit about me, but what really matters is that this person who has done these things is a man alive in Christ. I cannot speak because of what I have achieved or what I have done or who I am - only by what I have achieved and what I have done and who I am as I stand in Christ.

So the qualification for belonging to the Kingdom is that you are found in Christ. There are two supplementary questions. How are you found in Christ? You are found in Christ when you come to him. When you are born again of water and the Spirit. Jesus says, 'I tell you the truth, no-one can enter the Kingdom of God unless he is born of water and of the Spirit. Flesh gives birth to flesh but the Spirit gives birth to spirit. You should not be surprised at my saying "You must be born again." ' (vv.5-8) The tables have turned. The urbane, gracious, utterly in-control-of- himself theologian Nicodemus is now put on the spot by Jesus. Jesus is saying, *'Nicodemus, you ought to know these things. You ought to know that belonging to the Kingdom is to do with the new birth. The new birth is not some new-fangled idea; it is in your scriptures. Nicodemus, you are a theologian. You know the Old Testament. You have read Ezekiel 36? Nicodemus, do you understand that the living God says to the nations "I will sprinkle you with water and you shall be clean, and I will put my Spirit upon you and give you a new heart? - a heart of flesh, not a heart of stone." (vv.24-27) Nicodemus, do you understand that in the Old Testament God was saying to his people "You need a new birth, of water and the Spirit." Nicodemus, you must be born again.'*

I want to ask you, 'Are you in the Kingdom of God tonight? Have you been born again of water and the Spirit?' The Spirit is primary and the water is secondary. (v 8,9) The water is the outward sign bestowed upon those who have the inward reality but the two belong together like the two sides of a coin. You cannot really sensibly have the one without the other. There is no such thing in the New Testament as an unbaptised Christian. So, I want to ask you, where do you stand? Many people are indeed born again of the Spirit of God and that is primary, that is key. But if you are, have you been baptised? If you have not, you had better get on with it because it does not make any sense to be born again but not to be baptised. Two people came to me this morning after I had preached this sermon and said they want to get baptised; you need to join the queue. So if anyone here tonight belongs to Christ and has not been baptised, you need that outward confirmation, that sign to all the world of your visible participation in the body of Christ. On the other hand there are people who have been baptised by water but not by the Spirit of God. They are formal members on paper of the Church but they do not know Christ. Is that your position tonight? Do not rely on your water baptism alone to get you into the Kingdom. You must be born again. You must be a new creation. You must be incorporated into Christ. You must have opened your life to his presence. So qualification for entry to the Kingdom is that we stand in Christ, through new birth by water and the Spirit.

Then the second supplementary question. How then does the new birth come about? The answer is that it comes about through belief in Christ. From verse 11 onwards Jesus addresses the Jews who are gathered around. He talks about the presence of Christ, who has come down from God to the world and who is to be lifted up before the world on the cross for the world's salvation. To be a disciple, to be born again, to be a member of the Kingdom, to have eternal life (they all mean the same thing), you have to believe in Christ who came down from heaven as God incarnate and who was lifted up upon the cross to die for your sin. It is only when we turn from our selfishness, our self-will, our determination to save ourselves and we look to the cross that we are saved. We don't often preach basic, evangelistic sermons in St Saviour's but the text requires it and it might just be for you tonight. Have you been born again? That is not a fanatical, over-the-top religious question, it is deeply biblical. It is not even just New Testament, it is Old Testament. Have you been born again by the Spirit of God? Do you know you have been born again because you have come to put your faith in Christ, incarnate, crucified and risen? Jesus uses an illustration from the Old Testament story of Moses and the bronze snake which was raised on a pole so that anyone bitten by a real snake could look to the bronze image and live. (Numbers 21:5-8) So, as we look to Christ lifted up on the cross we are saved. Can I ask you, have you ever knelt at the cross, looked at Christ, accepted his sacrifice for your sin, and offered him your life?

> *He died that we might be forgiven,*
> *He died to make us good,*
> *That we might go at last to heaven*
> *Saved by his precious blood.*

In one sense I don't care about your status or achievements; you may be a Vicar, you may be a Bishop, you may have three theological degrees, you may be at the top of your profession. I don't care! All I care about is that you are a sinner who has looked to Christ and been redeemed.

Let's recap. First, what is the Kingdom? Second, who qualifies for entry? And now to our final Kingdom question: **What is the alternative to being in the Kingdom?** Listen carefully. The alternative to being in the Kingdom is not to be in the Kingdom. Well, well. How profound is that? What is the most famous verse in the Bible? Those of a certain age would immediately reply, 'Please sir, John 3:16: "God so loved the world that he gave his only begotten Son that whoever believed in him should not perish but have eternal life." ' In his Epistle John makes this even clearer. He says 'He who has the Son has life; he who has not the

Son of God does not have life.' (1 John 5.12) What bit of that sentence do you not understand? The heart of the Gospel is the boundless love of God for every man, woman and child - to be received or to be rejected.

So John ends by moving from the image of love to light. Jesus is the light of the world. He explains to the theologian standing before him that the natural default position of human beings is to stand in the darkness. It is easier to do wrong than to do right. (Consider any two-year-old that you know.) It's called 'original sin.' Jesus tells Nicodemus that the reason why people walk away from the light is that they are evil and they do not want the light to expose their doings. Why do people reject Christ? A thousand and one reasons are offered. Intellectual doubts, the problem of suffering, a rotten vicar ten years ago who would not baptise their baby. The real reason, the deepest reason, is that we do not want to come into the light. Coming to Christ means a moral transformation and most people do not want that. They want to live in darkness, either in the darkness of their wickedness, or in the darkness of their determination to save themselves by their own efforts. I am being very blunt tonight. It is a matter of light and darkness and we are invited to come into the light.

So finally, 'What can you see?' I am fascinated by verse 3. Jesus replies to Nicodemus 'I will tell you the truth, no-one can **see** the Kingdom of God unless he is born again.' It is to do with seeing. It is to do with looking. Looking at the serpent, looking at the cross. What, tonight, can you see? Most of us see what we want to see. It is only as Jesus opens our eyes that we know the truth.

> *Pussycat, pussycat, where have you been?*
> *I've been to London to see the Queen.*
> *Pussycat, pussycat, what saw you there?*
> *I saw a little mouse under her chair.*

The pussycat faced with the Queen of England could only see a mouse under a chair. Why? Because a cat has not the capacity to understand royalty, and, secondly, a cat is only interested in its next meal. Great theology in a nursery-rhyme! Your sight is limited and you see what you want to see.

Jesus says *'Nicodemus, I have come to open your eyes.'* Nicodemus came to Jesus by night. John never wastes a word. It's not just, *'Oh well, it's teatime, I'll go now, before it gets too dark.'* John is making a theological point. As Judas left the upper room to betray Jesus we read 'he went out and it was night.' Night in the soul of Judas; night in the soul of Nicodemus. I have just had this thought: I wonder whether Jesus and Nicodemus (on the Mount of Olives) talked through the night. I would not be surprised. Jesus had that capacity to stay with people. Perhaps they talked until the dawn began to break on the mountainside and as the light filtered through the trees did Nicodemus, hesitantly, carefully turn his face to the light of the world, never to be the same again? (John 19.38). Tonight the light is still shining from Christ the Lord through his word and I pray that you may face the light. Allow it to search you and humble you and redeem you so that you can go away today saying 'I belong to the Kingdom of God.' May it be so for Jesus' sake.

Amen

View from the Pew

'So to Ashted Church, where we had a dull Doctor, one Downe, worse than I think Parson King was, of whom we made so much scorn, and after sermon home, and staid while our dinner, a couple of large chickens, were dressed, and a good mess of cream.' Samuel Pepys 1663.

Samuel Pepys was clearly unimpressed by the sermon he heard 350 years ago mercifully my listening experience has been rather better

Here are some key ingredients that, for me, make a good sermon.

1. Shape. *There needs to be a beginning, middle and end.*
2. Direction. *A clear sense of where the sermon is going is vital.*
3. Intimacy. *It needs to be spoken from the heart and with a clear message that impacts on my life. I want to be addressed directly.*
4. Challenge. *It must rouse me from my complacency and challenge my thinking and actions during the week.*
5. Simplicity. *But also profound, often with clear 'bullet points' to aid the memory.*
6. Humour. *Liberally sprinkled but never forced.*
7. Quotations. *These often help to illustrate a point but must not be there to cover up a lack of understanding of the message.*
8. Practical advice. *Rooted in the real world with examples as to how the passage and its interpretation will help me live in a more godly way.*
9. Passion. *There must be passion in the delivery which comes from the preacher's own sense of engagement. My Vicar reminds me of Alan Bennett, whose delivery I can listen to till the cows come home!*
10. Biblically based. *Always rooted in the Scriptures and helpfully cross-referenced where appropriate.*
11. Engagement. *A sermon needs to be delivered so that I am unaware of the passage of time.*
12. Spirit-led. *'Were not our hearts burning within us while he talked with us on the road and opened the Scriptures to us?'*

Ian Cunliffe

Confession time!

The 'I am' sermon actually preached in this series was from John 11: 'I am the Resurrection and the Life.' But when I got the script typed from the sermon the structure was so poor that I was confused – not to say ashamed. I was just grateful I didn't have to listen to it when it was preached. It would have needed major reconstructive surgery and I decided instead to compose a sermon on another saying: 'I am the Light of the world.'

However, it is a salutary lesson in the need to check and re-check the flow of a sermon before preaching it! I hope this one works better. If it doesn't perhaps you could let me know.

22. Knocking holes in the darkness

Jesus said, 'I am the Light of the World.' The saying is comfortingly familiar and satisfyingly complete. Everyone knows what light is. No-one – except maybe a few scientists – can describe it. But we all know what it does. Earlier, in the magnificent prologue John had written, 'In him (Christ) was life and the life was the light of men. The light shines in the darkness, and the darkness has not overcome it.' And later, he was to write 'God is light and in him is no darkness at all.' (1 John 1:5) This morning we come to one of the famous 'I am's' of John's Gospel. In one sense these sayings stand alone, simple and complete: 'I am the light of the world,' 'I am the bread of life,' and 'I am the good Shepherd.' But if we really want to understand their meaning we must pay careful attention to the context.

Jesus makes this claim during the annual Jewish Feast of Tabernacles (7:2) in which Israel's experience of being led through the wilderness by the provision of supernatural light is commemorated (Ex 13:21). Four enormous golden candlesticks were lit, and their light was said to shine across the whole night sky of Jerusalem. At the end of the Feast as the lights are ready to be extinguished, Jesus stands in the Temple and says 'I am the light of the world.' The blazing lights of the candelabra (75' high!) illuminate Jerusalem for a brief moment. Jesus is claiming to bring light to the whole world – for ever! It is a bold claim.

So, what does it mean to say that Jesus is the light of the world? It all depends of course on where you are standing. If, this morning, you intentionally bring yourself into that light, the claim of Jesus **will fill you with gratitude.** 'I am the light of the world. Whoever follows me will never walk in darkness, but will have the light of life.' In the darkness, we are prone to stumble and fall; in the light we move with confidence. Which would you prefer? Suddenly there's a power cut and it goes completely dark in your house. Unless you are a member of one of those irritating households who have a torch (with a battery fitted and operative) close to hand for such an emergency, you grope around wondering where the matches have gone and whether you have any candles and if so where they might be. You stumble, you bump into bits of furniture, you are disorientated. Then, without warning, the lights come back on and order is restored to your world! You resolve to buy a torch – but of course you never do! To follow Christ is to walk with confidence and poise, one step at a time. Please note that the light of the world comes to each disciple, not as a searchlight cleaving the darkness for miles around, but more like a candle giving enough light just for the next step. There's a great verse in Psalm 18 which reads in an old translation as follows: 'Thou also shalt light my candle: the Lord my God shall make my darkness to be light.' (Psalm 18:28 AV) Isn't that good? And some of us can remember Cardinal Newman's marvellous hymn:

> *Lead kindly light,*
> *Amid th'encircling gloom,*
> *Lead thou me on;*
> *The night is dark,*
> *And I am far from home;*
> *Lead thou me on.*
> *Keep thou my feet;*
> *I do not ask to see*
> *The distant scene;*
> *One step enough for me.*
> (John Henry Newman, 1801-1890)

Our post-modern culture is chronically uncertain. We may be technologically sure-footed, but in the ordering of our personal and public morality we are all over the place. We stumble and fall.

Jesus said, 'I am the light of the world.' But if you turn away, or back yourself into a dark corner, the words of Jesus become a **threat and a judgement.** In chapter 9 John tells the dramatic story of the healing of a man who was born blind. The joy of this healing is overshadowed by the furious response of the Pharisees because the healing had happened on the Sabbath. They question the man, then they interrogate his parents, then they question him for a second time. The man is cock-a-hoop (you would be if you'd had your eyes opened for the first time ever) and refuses to be cowed. So the religious authorities drive him out of church (9:34). Jesus finds him and questions him – but he does so gently and creatively: 'Do you believe in the Son of Man?' 'I do' says the man, and he worships Jesus! Then John records these chilling words: 'Jesus said, "I am come into this world for judgement so that those who do not see may see, and those who do see may become blind." ' (9:39) It's a marvellous story and I've almost begun another sermon. Sorry! A sermon within a sermon: the stuff of nightmares!

But the point is this. Light received brings hope and confidence, light rejected condemns us to live in the darkness. Why would we choose to live in darkness? Well, the answer to that is in another passage of this Gospel where Jesus is talking to Nicodemus. 'And this is the judgement, that the light has come into the world, and people loved darkness rather than light because their deeds were evil. For all who love evil hate the light and do not come to the light....' (3.19-20). We looked at this passage last week – do you remember? No! What a disappointment you are to me! We are dangerously free to turn away from Christ, to rely on the fragile light of our own philosophies, to follow the fading illumination of our own ambitions, to walk in the darkness of unbelief. Please do not go that way. It will end in tears.

Open yourself today to the clean, pure light of the presence of Christ. Let that light search you, unmask your darkness, heal you, restore you and then guide you all your days. I have followed that light for fifty years now, sometimes falteringly, often reluctantly, but it has never been extinguished, it has never led me astray. Jesus said 'Whoever follows me shall never walk in darkness...' It's true!

The light which directs our way, or condemns our waywardness, is the light we share with a darkened world. This saying is a promise and a warning, but finally it is a challenge. Jesus said, 'I am the light of the world,' but he also said to his followers, 'You are the light of the world...' (Matt 5.14) The light we have received is the light we bear to others that they too may walk with confidence.

When the novelist Robert Louis Stevenson was a little boy, he was standing one day at the window of his nursery in the family home in Edinburgh. On the street below was the lamplighter, with his ladder and taper, lighting the gas lamps one by one. 'What are you doing?' said the nurse to the little boy. 'Watching that man knocking holes in the darkness' was the reply.[1]

Jesus said, 'I am the light of the world.' What a comfort that is! Jesus also said, 'You are the light of the world.' What a challenge that is! Are you up for it? I trust so. Let's go and do it together.

> *Spirit of truth and love,*
> *Life-giving holy Dove,*
> *Speed forth thy flight;*
> *Move on the water's face*
> *Bearing the lamp of grace*
> *And in earth's darkest place*
> *Let there be light.*
> (John Marriott, 1780-1825)

1. I am aware that I used this illustration in an earlier sermon (No.14) but to a different congregation. If things work we should not be afraid of repeating them!

The vicar asked people to switch
off their mobile phones

I find John 17 a daunting chapter.

John records the prayer of Jesus and, instinctively, we know we are on holy ground. I wonder how he came to hear it?

The first part of the sermon is quite compressed, but if taken slowly I think it makes sense. However I felt it necessary to make a special effort to root the theological concept in practical Christian discipleship – hence the two fairly detailed stories which make up the second half of the sermon.

I'm not sure this makes for a well balanced sermon, but it felt right at the time. But care does have to be taken with stories lest they run away with themselves.

My wife sometimes says, 'Nice story – what were you trying to say?'

23.What Jesus wants
for his Church

Down the corridor of the Church Centre in the room occupied by two of my colleagues, Debbie and Julian, I have my files of sermons going back over 40 years. They cover a whole wall! I looked up John 17 and found in it one sermon preached in May 1983 in my last church. I couldn't make head or tail of it, but that's another issue! I was shocked that over 40 years I have only preached once on this magnificent passage. I don't know why that is. It may be one shies away from it because we are standing on holy ground. William Temple, in his majestic commentary on John's Gospel, says that this chapter is the most important in all the Gospels.[1] In chapters 14-16 Jesus has been discoursing in the upper room with his disciples about the nature of their union with him, about the state of the world that opposes them, and about the gift of the Holy Spirit. In chapter 18 the trial begins and the narrative moves swiftly to the cross and resurrection. In between is chapter 17, what is known as 'The High Priestly Prayer.' On the night before he was betrayed Jesus prays. He prays first for his own relationship with the Father (vv.1-5), then he prays for the disciples (vv.6-19), and then he prays for all believers (vv.20-26). He prays for the church present and future, he prays for the church represented by his little band of disciples and he prays for all believers who are yet to come. And we are here today because those first disciples told what they knew. They told the story and the story was passed from generation to generation. And after us there will be future generations. So it has been said that the church is always one generation from extinction.

How do we get into this astonishing passage in 20 minutes? Well, the passage seems to be answering this question: 'What does Jesus want for his Church?' I have one sermon on John 17 but come to my study and I could show you at least two dozen books on the church, what it is, why it is failing, how it can succeed and so on. Perhaps I should sell them and just concentrate on John 17 because John 17 answers the question: 'What does Jesus want for his church?' But there is a prior question, linked to it, embedded in the text and in the prayer. 'What is the Church?' And the answer, (vv.6-8) is that it is the company of those God has called out of the world and given to Jesus for his protection. These people have done three things. They have accepted the word of God, that is, they have accepted the rule and authority of God over the world. They have come to understand that the nature and purpose of God is revealed in the face of Jesus Christ. The result is that they have put active trust in the Father and in the Son by the power of the Holy Spirit. These are the people who are called from the world to be the Church. On that basis, are you a member of the Church? Does this not make your pulse race? We have been called out of the world, marked by Father, Son and Holy Spirit, given eternal life, protected for time and eternity but then sent back into the world to proclaim in our time the goodness of God. If that doesn't get your pulse racing I don't know what would!

Now we are ready for our main question: 'What does Jesus want for his Church?' Please listen very carefully. The glory that is shared between Father and Son is poured into the people of God and that glory within them causes them to have a unity of purpose and mind which is expressed in a lifestyle of joy and love which will cause a watching world to believe. Did you get that? No, I thought not. Gordon, please keep concentrating!

Let's unpack it for a few moments. There are four key words: glory, unity, joy and love. Glory is a fundamental biblical word. It is the word that summarises all that God is in his nature and being, his beauty, power, love, grace and so on, and the honour that is due to him because of who he is. So glory is poured out in the Godhead between the Father and the Son. Glory is not the honour that God takes to himself, but an honour he shares with the Son. The Son displays that glory and reflects it back to the Father in an act of perfect unity. And then, says Jesus, that glory is poured out upon the people of God, we become partakers of the divine glory. The Spirit draws us into the magnetic field of the glory of the Father and the Son. All that God is, is poured out upon his people, and our unity simply consists in being held together in the gravitational pull of the Godhead's glory. So unity is not something that we work for, it is something that is given. Our job is to make that unity real, and there is no logical reason why what is true at a theological level should not ultimately be true at a practical level in the way the Church lives out its corporate life. No reason, apart from our sinfulness! So the ultimate scandal of the Church is our tragic disunity. But through the clouds of our failure we glimpse from time to time a shaft of light, we catch sight of that unity God intends. Suddenly it breaks through the walls of division that hold us apart and we say, 'Yes, that is what it's about.' You go across the world and you meet a Christian radiant with Christ and there is immediately a sense of being united. You don't have to start discussing what school you went to and whether you share common interests; you are united in Christ, across all barriers.

So glory brings unity and the overflow of unity is joy and love (v.13). Joy is a deep awareness that we are held in life and death in the hands of God, Father, Son and Holy Spirit. That is where our joy comes from. It does not come from our bank balance. It does not come from the weather, it does not come from the hope of a good holiday. That is happiness which is dependent on shifting circumstances. Joy is our rootedness in God which enables us to stand firm and calm and wonderfully alive, whatever may be going on around. And then of course the love which flows from the Father and the Son is poured into our hearts (v.23 and v.26). There isn't time to look at this. Go home, put the lunch on hold and read John 17. It is breathtaking! Then finally, when the Church receives the glory of God and is united in a display of joy and love, the world will see and believe that God sent Jesus Christ to be the Saviour of the world. As Jesus prepares to go to the cross his thoughts are on the Church as the instrument of reconciliation for the whole world.

So where does all this theology leave us on this hot Sunday morning? Come on Vicar, give us something to hold onto! Here are two stories as a reward for listening so far - although I've seen one or two people yawning over on the right. Yesterday I found myself in a conversation with a young man who is on the cusp of offering for ordination into the Anglican church. He has to write an essay as part of his application process. And he asked me to reflect on what is important to me after forty years of ministry. Sometimes, you know, the things that you find yourself saying when you are put on the spot are actually the things you most deeply believe. And I found myself talking about unity, about the essentials that passionately matter to me. I said the essentials are big, but there aren't many of them. Belief in the Lordship of Jesus Christ, Son of the Father, the indwelling presence of the Holy Spirit, salvation by grace through faith, the call to bear witness in the world to the truth of the Gospel. These are the things that matter, and with not a lot of time left (but a few years, I hope) I am more and more aware of the things that unite and less and less inclined to spend precious energy patrolling the boundaries of my detailed convictions. Our task is to show a broken world that Jesus is alive – that is what fires me, more and more. Some might say I'm becoming vague and easy-going. So be it. My desire is to be focussed, honed and passionate. If the prayer of Jesus is a plea for unity of purpose, the question that remains (and what every sermon ought to address) is 'What do we do?'

So to my second story. Yesterday I went to the Cathedral for Phil Mann's[2] priesting and you know my track record with Cathedral protocol. Well, it's happened again. I arrived slightly late with my robes bundled under my arm and I rushed down the south transept to find myself being advanced upon by two processions, with a verger carrying a huge cross. I dodged to the side as the first procession swept by. There were clergy from St Saviour's in it, all looking a bit smug, I thought. No sooner had I recovered than another procession came, with all the ordination candidates in it; some of them grinned at me in an unhelpful sort of way! In growing desperation I ran to the chapter house and there, to my enormous relief, I found some clergy who had not yet got into a procession. They were the Canons and they said 'Canon Bracewell, you are just in time, you are in the Canons' procession.' Wow! Big time. So I got into my procession and one of the Canons said to me 'You know those electronic things on bus shelters which give you journey details, we should have one here that says 'The next procession is leaving in two minutes and is bound for the high altar via the west end.' The whole thing is ridiculous in a hilarious Anglican sort of way. And we all get on with it, because that's what we do.

But then we came to the sermon, and the preacher was talking about the nature of the Church and he was saying that so often we are tempted to turn the Church into a pale imitation of secular organisation (St Saviour's plc). But in reality the Church is simply a company of broken people offering help to other broken people. And he used the example of L'Arche community in France which embraces and takes into itself those who are disabled, those whom the world often thinks of no account. He challenged us to think small, to think counter-culturally, to think like Jesus. For me it was a powerful moment: when all is said and done (and an awful lot is said and done in the Church!) all we have to do is to go out tomorrow morning and reach one more broken person with the truth of Christ. You can manage that, can't you? John Wesley records in his journal the occasion when he stood on a hillside outside Bristol. Around him hundreds of miners had gathered. He records that their tears were making rivulets down their dust-caked faces as they heard the good news of the Gospel. 'For the space of two hours I offered them Christ' he wrote. Isn't that wonderful? We may not be able to take in all the theology of John 17 this lunchtime (but please try) – but may God give us grace to go out and offer Christ.

1. William Temple, 'Readings in St John's Gospel', (Macmillan & Co Ltd, 1961).
2. Phil Mann, our Youth Pastor and my son-in-law.

View from the Pew

'Man does not live by bread alone, but on every word that comes from the mouth of God' (Matthew 4.4). A good sermon, then, should be like a freshly baked loaf of bread, still warm, so that it seems to come straight from the preacher's heart, and filled with whole-grains of God's truth.

So what is the recipe for the perfect sermon? First of all, and above all, a sermon should be scriptural. Full of the wholesome wheat of God's word, carefully separated from the chaff of popular opinion and the wisdom of the world. A sermon is not an opinion-piece; we can read plenty of those in the Sunday papers.

A sermon should also be substantial, not necessarily long, but with a clear spiritual aim, and a carefully thought-out theme. Just as perfectly good wheat can be pumped full of air and end up as a bowl of puffed wheat (no, thank you !), so a sermon can have a faintly scriptural flavour, but no nutritious substance. God's word.

There should be a good structure. To become a loaf of bread, a lump of dough is put into a tin to give it shape; clearly defined points and helpful signposts to keep him on track; alliteration can help here – if not overdone!

An important ingredient is salt. Paul tells the Colossians (4.6) that their conversation should be 'seasoned with salt' – and the Latin for 'conversation' is 'sermo'! A sermon should convey the word of God, but should also express the humanity of the preacher: a sermon is not a Reith Lecture! A preacher should certainly give us spiritual directions for our journey through life, but not with the impersonal omniscience of a sat. nav.!

One vital ingredient remains. Bread without yeast is just a lifeless lump of dough, and a sermon is just empty words and wasted breath unless it is given life and power by God's Holy Spirit. Only if the Holy Spirit is breathing his life into a sermon will it truly be the Word of God.

The recipe for the perfect sermon? No sermon, humanly speaking, is perfect; but, as they say, half a loaf is better than no bread!

Cary Gilbart-Smith

For the past four years the four congregations of St Saviour's have come together for an annual service of celebration in Guildford Cathedral.

We have a picnic lunch on the lawn at the West End of the Cathedral where (in theory) we mingle and meet new people, and then at 2pm we gather in the vast, beautifully light building to worship.

Setting up our own sound system and musicians is a technical (and financial!) challenge but well worth it. They have proved to be moving occasions and somehow being together for that short space of time seems to have an uplifting effect quite out of proportion to the time spent.

This simple expression of unity seems to energise us for the next phase of our life as a church. Everyone loves it and it is now a firmly established tradition.

On this occasion Victor Stock, the Dean, was on study leave, so we were hosted by Canon Jonathan Frost, Residentiary Canon, University Chaplain and a good friend of St Saviour's.

24. Abundant Life

Last week, Brian Caswell of Bolton won £25m on the Euro Lottery.[1] He works on an allotment just behind where I used to live as a boy. Perhaps I should write and ask if he remembers me! In the same newspaper I learned that Julian Lloyd Webber is preparing to marry for the fourth time. Recently a friend of mine has been given the hint that he might well be in line for a bishopric.

In what does Abundant Life consist? Material wealth, stable relationships, career advancement? Maybe, maybe not. As God's people we want to say that 'abundant life' flows from knowing God in Christ. The key text that lies behind the experience is John 10:10. Jesus says 'I have come that they may have life, and have it to the full.' This full life is nothing other than God's life within the human heart. 'I give them eternal life and they shall never perish.' (John 10:29)

The problem, of course, about 10:10 is that it is embedded in quite a complex passage about sheep and shepherds and sheepfolds and robbers. Jesus is talking about his care for people. It is, he explains, like a shepherd's care for his sheep. His hearers find it quite confusing. I like the 'Message' translation of verse 6: 'Jesus told this story, but they had no idea what he was talking about. So he tried again.' He talks about himself as the gate through which the sheep may safely pass, and about the false shepherds who gain unauthorised entry, bent only on destruction of the sheep. Then suddenly this glowing sentence about abundant life. Finally he develops the image of himself as the Good Shepherd. It's one of those biblical passages we think is simple and clear, but more detailed study uncovers complexity: always the case in John's Gospel, as in recent weeks we have seen!

In the few moments available let me draw out a few aspects of the abundant life that Christ the Good Shepherd imparts to his people.

It is a life of **security.** We are known, loved and led. The Good Shepherd calls his sheep by name, leads them out, goes ahead and they follow because they know his voice. To be known is to be loved; to be loved is to be known. And known and loved we can move through a dangerous and delightful world surefooted and secure. This is the high privilege of the Christian disciple, but at the same time a deep responsibility. The last thing you can say about our post-modern culture is that it is surefooted. Beneath the fear, the confusion and the cynicism, people are looking for a clear lead to follow. What a challenge to the church!

Secondly, abundant life is a life of **hospitality.** 'I have other sheep that are not of this sheep pen. I must bring them also. They too will listen to my voice, and there shall be one flock and one shepherd.'" (John 10:16) The sheep pen is not an enclosed place, it is open to continual expansion. At the heart of our security there is a vulnerability which will never allow us to settle down in cosy self-sufficiency. The Church of Jesus Christ is by definition a mission community and whenever that vision fades it can soon unravel into a religious club and then death is not far away. Archbishop William Temple said 'The Church is the only organisation that exists solely for the benefit of its non-members.' When Victor Stock first came to the Cathedral he began to open up the doors that had long been bolted and barred, as a physical sign of the opening up of the community here. On one occasion he was approached by an exasperated lady about the unlocking of the door on the south side of the building. 'Why,' said Victor, with that guileless innocence of his, 'Why should we not unlock it?' To which the lady replied 'People will come in!' Jesus said: 'I have other sheep – I must bring them also.'

Thirdly, abundant life is a life of **freedom.** Jesus says that whoever comes to him will be saved and will come in and go out and find pasture. (John 10:9) Being saved through Christ we can come and go. Abundant life sets us free and keeps us on the move, ever discovering new experiences, new challenges, new avenues of service. In Christ our minds are stimulated, our eyes are opened to the beauty and tragedy of his world, our hearts are melted by what we see and our imaginations are set on fire with all the potential for change that lies before us.

Finally, there is **vision**. The writer to the Hebrews describes the risen Christ as 'that great Shepherd of the sheep' and prays that we will be equipped to live well as his followers. The description comes in a passage at the end of the letter, focussed on urging Christians to keep going, never to give up or drop out of the Christian pilgrimage. So abundant life is a life of visionary purpose which will keep us on track. Disciples never retire, they believe crazily that all things are possible.

Some time ago one of my students sent me an email:

> *At a nursing home a resident group was discussing ailments:*
> *'My arms are so weak I can hardly lift this cup of coffee' said one.*
> *'Yes, I know, my cataracts are so bad I can't even see my coffee' replied another.*
> *'I can't turn my head because of the arthritis in my neck' said a third, at which several others nodded weakly.*
> *'My blood pressure pills make me very dizzy' another went on.*
> *'I guess that's the price we pay for getting old' winced an old man.*
> *There was general agreement and a short moment of silence ensued.*
> *'Well, it's not that bad' said one woman cheerfully. 'Thank God we can all still drive!'*

So, as Sue and I move on to a new phase of ministry and as you, our dear flock, await your new pastor, may we all be found fruitful until that day when '...the Lamb at the centre of the throne will be (our) shepherd, and he will lead (us) to springs of living water, and God will wipe away every tear from (our) eyes.' (Rev 7:17)

1. The sermon was preached on Sunday 21st June 2009